JOHN ANTHONY

ONCE *for* ALL

Learning God's Nature

Once For All: Learning God's Nature
Book 1
by John Anthony

Signalman Publishing
www.signalmanpublishing.com
email: info@signalmanpublishing.com
Kissimmee, Florida

Copyright © 2012 by John Anthony Giudice. All rights reserved. No part of this book may be reproduced or transmitted in any form or by any means, electronic or mechanical, or incorporated into any information retrieval system, electronic or mechanical, without the written permission of the copyright owner.

ISBN: 978-1-935991-77-9 (Paperback)
978-1-935991-78-6 (ebook)

Scripture quotations taken from the New American Standard Bible®, Copyright © 1960, 1962, 1963, 1968, 1971, 1972, 1973, 1975, 1977, 1995 by The Lockman Foundation
Used by permission.

Edited by Alice Scott

Typeset in Adobe Garamond Pro
Cover artwork created by Jean Giudice
Book design by Joel Ramnaraine

Library of Congress Control Number: 2012954638

TABLE OF CONTENTS

Introduction   5

Chapter 1	The Ancient Scriptures: The Word	7
Chapter 2	A Father to Us All	31
Chapter 3	Jesus Walked Among Us	48
Chapter 4	The Holy Spirit: The Comforter	93
Chapter 5	Faith of a Mustard Seed	114
Chapter 6	Only Believe	146
Chapter 7	Love Is Greater Than All	163
Chapter 8	Free Will: A Gift of Love	182

This book is dedicated to my family
and to all those searching for the truth.

INTRODUCTION

As a child, I was taught to appreciate the small things in life. This was easy for me because we didn't have much. Each year, my mother would hand my siblings and me a Sears and Roebuck catalog. She would open it to the section where we could pick out one gift for Christmas. That was it, one gift each year.

As I raced through the pictures, I would imagine each toy in my possession. Of course, the difficult part was choosing just one from the very limited selection from which we were allowed to choose. Needless to say, with this learned appreciation, I took very good care of everything I had.

By my parents' standards, my siblings and I were spoiled, even though we had so little. By my own standards as a parent, now, my children seem more spoiled than I was. With each successive generation, children have more and appreciate less.

The only way I can explain it is that we love our children so much, we want to give them in abundance the things we never had—or had very little of.

Guess what? Our heavenly Father feels the same way about us. He loves us so much He wants to spoil us with the riches of His love and grace. He also wants us to appreciate even the small things of life, not taking anything for granted. Our amazing God is *"...able to do far more abundantly beyond all that we ask or think"* (Ephesians 3:20), and yet how often do we see Him as a stern parent limiting our freedom to choose anything we want in life.

As you explore this book, I want you to look at the gifts on each page as if you were searching through that Sears and Roebuck catalog I mentioned earlier. You can do it with one major difference: you can choose any number of gifts from any page in the book—no limits.

That's what God offers us. He has given us the freedom to follow the paths of our own choosing to select as many gifts from the catalog of life as we desire. He wants us to choose wisely, because He knows that the decisions we make will not only shape the outcome of our lives here on earth, but will have the power to determine our eternal destiny.

Chapter 1

THE ANCIENT SCRIPTURES: THE WORD

In my early years as a youngster running through the woods of upstate New York or in later years exploring the mountains of Colorado and Wyoming, I acquired an appreciation of nature that has become part of me. I also came to understand that there is much more to the complexity of nature than our science books would have us believe. No matter how many times I've returned to familiar places, I would see things that were previously missed. Each visit would reap more knowledge and give me a sense of excitement when a new revelation was gained. For me, reading the Scriptures is not all that different because with each visit something new and exciting is revealed.

There is much I want to share about the Scriptures, not the least of which, is the profound affect that fully immersing myself in God's word has had on my life. First, I want to give you some historical background and interesting facts.

According to historians, the ancient documents of Scripture were recorded between 1500 BC and the first century AD. They are among the oldest documented writings in existence. Interestingly, they have been preserved not only in good physical condition, but also have been found in various places all over the world from different time periods and without any content changes. They are, in fact, the most complete historical, cultural, and spiritual accounting of the Israelite people.

The canon of Scripture, or what we have come to know as the Bible, includes 66 books, having 1,189 chapters and 810,697 words. They were written by more than 40 authors, from Genesis to Revelation. All the books of the Bible, both in the Old and New Testaments, contain God's word to us written by the prophets of old and devoted men who were led by the Spirit of God. To date, the Bible remains the most reproduced book in the history of man.

Story or Truth

Many of us have been raised to think of the Bible as a collection of stories that can be taken lightly, or not at all. We believe or disbelieve and leave the rest for the Sunday sermon. Each person's opinion or interpretation of the words can differ like night and day. However, I have found that opinions not grounded in the knowledge of the Word, are because it is read from a worldly perspective, thinking with logic and emotion, not from a spiritual sense.

Some of us have preconceived opinions. These opinions

are formed even though we may have never read the Bible in its entirety. Instead, we are being influenced by world views of family, friends, teachers, or perhaps our past experiences. However, the truth is there if you're interested. Maybe we don't want any restraints placed on our behavior, so we believe the lies in our willful blindness.

Do you believe there are absolute spiritual truths? For me it is clear. I don't believe the myth that "truth is in the eye of the beholder." I will agree we each have a perspective on life, but there are absolute spiritual truths just as there are physical truths in the world of science.

Take for instance gravity. This holds us to the ground. Or better yet that the earth is spinning while traveling on an orbit around our sun. We accept these truths taught by our science teachers in faith. We also accept the meanings of the hieroglyphics found in Egypt as factual and therefore, believe what we are taught in faith. Why is it then that we struggle with historical facts and the spiritual truths found throughout the Scriptures?

BE PREPARED

Yes, we all have our opinions about the Bible, that's for sure. But how can we justify our opinions or presume to be an authority without having actually read it? In fact, we may have deep emotions tied to our opinions. Where does that come from? You don't claim to be an authority on critical mountain climbing without first learning everything you can on the subject. You start with easy climbs, not tackling the "Diamond" on Longs Peak (Colorado), for instance, because your life depends on it. You don't become a math, history, or science professor without first taking classes and going through the process of meeting all of the requirements. Therefore, you must read, study and become familiar with the topic before you can claim an authoritative opinion if you're to be taken seriously.

Being imperfect, we learn we should be better prepared if we want to increase our chances for success. If we viewed the rules or warning signs seriously, we would minimize the pitfalls of making bad decisions. We would also avoid the pain associated with failure by diligently doing our homework. We would be wise to follow the old Boy Scout motto of "Be prepared" or the military Latin version "IN OMNIA PARATUS," which means "in all things prepare."

When I was a teenager, our family went on a picnic in the mountains of Colorado not far from our home. We enjoyed the outdoors and our mission was to explore the nearby mountain. At the end of the day, my father yelled to us, "It's time to go home. Get down here!" Instead of taking the safe way down which was longer, I decided to throw my rope over a large protruding rock on the edge of a small 35 foot cliff and climb down the rope. As I lowered myself, I felt the rope slacken. I surmised that the rock I slung the rope over was coming dislodged from the cliff. Having my toes on a small ledge, and without looking up at the rock, I instinctively made the split second decision to jump off backwards doing a complete 360 and landed on my hands and knees like a cat.

Fortunately, the five ton boulder missed me and slammed into the earth at the base of the cliff. Upon impact, it broke in two. Half of it planted itself firmly there, while the other half crashed down the steep slope with a deafening sound, snapping small trees on its way to the bottom. I hadn't tested the rock beforehand to insure it was viable and therefore was not prepared for the resultant near death experience.

When your life is at risk, I don't have to tell you that it's foolish not to explore all the possibilities of what could go wrong before you blindly move forward. The same reasoning should be applied to decisions you make concerning your life.

None of us know how long we will live, but are we prepared for what happens after death? Even those that believe there is no life after death should at least consider all the possibilities. If they're wrong, they may find themselves at a distinct disadvantage.

God Breathed

All Scripture is inspired by God, yes written by men, but inspired and guided by God. We see evidence of this in 2 Timothy 3:16:

All Scripture is inspired by God and profitable for teaching, for reproof, for correction, for training in righteousness; that the man of God may be adequate, equipped for every good work.

And again we read the words written in 2 Peter 1:20:

> *But know this first of all, that no prophecy of Scripture is a matter of one's own interpretation, for no prophecy was ever made by an act of human will, but men moved by the Holy Spirit spoke from God.*

All Scripture is the Word of God. The emphasis is on the word "*All.*" If you don't believe this, then anything written can be dismissed at a whim. If any one thing can be questioned or dismissed as impossible or questionable, then everything is subject to the same dismissal. Furthermore, if you don't believe that all Scripture is the Word of God, you are being deceived by the enemy. There is no question or doubt in my mind, every word written was chosen by God for His specific purpose. It was given to men to record so everyone would benefit from them by gaining answers to all of our questions.

THE WORD IS LIVING

The Word of God is "living," in that as we grow in the Spirit, we will gain more wisdom and therefore more understanding with each visit. Like the layers of an onion, verses revisited with the help of the Holy Spirit, further reveal more useful knowledge. The more I read the Word, the more knowledge I gain, and the more I gain, the more I realize just how much practical life-altering information the Bible contains; it's almost overwhelming. To understand all that God has communicated to us throughout the chapters and verses of the Bible will seemingly take a life time of life times to learn.

In the book of Hebrews (4:12) we read:

For the Word of God is living and active and sharper than any two-edged sword, and piercing as far as the division of soul and spirit, of both joints and marrow, and able to judge the thoughts and intentions of the heart.

Every word of every verse has meaning and it's placement in the verse has purpose. As we grow in the Spirit we will see this and will slow down reading in order to analyze the chapter, verse or even why a specific word was used. We might even go back to the original Hebrew (Old Testament) or Greek (New Testament) to learn their meaning for a better understanding. We will come to learn there is truth and power in the Word of God beyond our comprehension causing us to trust and rely more in Him.

Without immersing ourselves in the Scriptures, we will become stagnant. We will not experience spiritual growth. Without realizing it, we will be more easily deceived and blinded by the world views that lead to separation from God and the truths that abound in the Scriptures.

HOLY SPIRIT REVEALS TRUTH

Just as the prophets and authors of the Scriptures were, *"… moved by the Holy Spirit spoke from God"* (2 Peter 1:20), we cannot understand the Scripture unless the Holy Spirit is in our heart. To those reading the words of Scripture without the Holy Spirit in their heart appear to be foolishness and without meaning—or like nonsense. Yet to those seeking truth, each word has meaning and each word has a place in time to be revealed by the Holy Spirit.

We may not always agree or understand with what has been recorded, but in time all things will be understood if you truly want to know the truth and the Holy Spirit reveals it to you. This is evidenced in the writing found in 1 Corinthians, chapter 2:10-16:

> *For to us God revealed them through the Spirit; for the Spirit searches all things, even the depths of God. For who among men knows the thoughts of a man except the spirit of the man which is in Him? Even so the thoughts of God no one knows except the Spirit of God. Now we have received, not the spirit of the world, but the Spirit who is from God, so that we may know the things freely given to us by God, which things we also speak, not in words taught by human wisdom, but in those taught by the Spirit, combining spiritual thoughts with spiritual words.*

You see, we can't understand the words of God if we don't have the Spirit of God in our heart. Take for instance what Paul recorded in Romans chapter 1:16-25 (caps represent quoted Old Testament Scripture):

> *For I am not ashamed of the gospel, for it is the power of God for salvation to everyone who believes, to the Jew first and also to the Greek.*
>
> *For in it the righteousness of God is revealed from*

*faith to faith; as it is written, "*B*UT THE* R*IGHTEOUS MAN SHALL LIVE BY FAITH.*" *For the wrath of God is revealed from heaven against all ungodliness and unrighteousness of men, who suppress the truth in unrighteousness, because that which is known about God is evident within them; for God made it evident to them.*

For since the creation of the world His invisible attributes, His eternal power and divine nature, have been clearly seen, being understood through what has been made, so that they are without excuse. For even though they knew God, they did not honor Him as God, or give thanks; but they became futile in their speculations, and their foolish heart was darkened.

Professing to be wise, they became fools, and exchanged the glory of the incorruptible God for an image in the form of corruptible man and of birds and four-footed animals and crawling creatures. Therefore, God gave them over in the lusts of their hearts to impurity, that their bodies might be dishonored among them… For they exchanged the truth of God, for a lie, and worshiped and served the creature rather than Creator, who is blessed forever.

This speaks of those lost in the worldly mindset versus those who are eagerly seeking truth and recognize that God is the Creator of all things. We must get our heart right, so that we may see with our eyes and hear with our ears the truth that abounds within the verses of the Bible. Otherwise, we will not have the desire to read it, nor will we understand it when we do read it.

In countless places throughout the Bible, God speaks of the eyes, ears and heart being closed or hardened. When we turn away from God and fix our eyes on the world, God actually allows our hearts to be hardened and our spiritual eyes and ears are closed as a result. This should not come as a shock to you because we have free will to choose our own direction even if that takes us away from Him.

Yes, in His love for us, He has gifted us with the freedom to reject Him if we so desire. He doesn't want robots following after Him. But when we do return to Him, He has promised to heal us. We should all take solace in this.

THE WORD IS TIMELESS

I believe the Scriptures apply to today as much as they did in the time they were written, making them timeless. This is evidenced to the many places in the New Testament that refer to the words recorded in the Old Testament, making them pertinent in the present sense in that day.

Here are words that help explain the timelessness of God's word in Isaiah 40:8, *"The grass withers, the flower fades, but the word of God stands forever."*

We also read that the word of God is tested in Proverbs 30:5, *"Every word of God is tested; He is a shield to those who take refuge in Him."*

And finally, in the book of Mathew (4:4) we read the words of Jesus, *"It is written, 'Man shall not live on bread alone, but on every word that proceeds out of the mouth of God.'"*

Parables of the Scriptures

Jesus often spoke in parables. This left people puzzled by His words. There were times that He explained the meaning to His disciples, but not always. When His disciples asked Him why He spoke in parables, He offered this explanation which was recorded in Mathew 13:13-15 (caps represent Old Testament Scripture always):

> *Therefore, I speak to them in parables; because while seeing they do not see, and while hearing they do not hear, nor do they understand. And in their case the prophecy of Isaiah is being fulfilled, which says,*
>
> "YOU WILL KEEP ON HEARING, BUT WILL NOT UNDERSTAND;
>
> AND YOU WILL KEEP ON SEEING; BUT WILL NOT PERCEIVE;
>
> FOR THE HEART OF THIS PEOPLE HAS BECOME DULL,
>
> AND WITH THEIR EARS THEY SCARCELY HEAR,
>
> AND THEY HAVE CLOSED THEIR EYES
>
> LEST THEY SHOULD SEE WITH THEIR EYES,
>
> AND HEAR WITH THEIR EARS,
>
> AND UNDERSTAND WITH THEIR HEART AND RETURN,
>
> AND I SHOULD HEAL THEM."

Jesus also told that us that He blesses those who have turned back to Him in Mathew 13:16-17:

> *But blessed are your eyes, because they see; and your ears, because they hear. For truly I say to you, that many*

prophets and righteous men desired to see what you see, and did not see it; and to hear what you hear, and did not hear it.

We often give examples or analogies to better explain the point we are trying to make. However, we seldom speak in parables, unless we want to limit who will understand. Similarly, Jesus is saying the same thing with the difference being those would never understand because their hearts are hardened to the truth. In other words, their hearts were far from Him, being lost in the world.

We also know that even those close to Him were puzzled by His use of parables. I believe He wanted them to earnestly desire understanding. He also wanted to discourage the lazy learner seeking knowledge; those that wanted it handed to them on a silver platter, so to speak, without having to work for it. Anyone who gets something without working will never appreciate it.

Take for instance gold miners in search of the perfect vein. If they were lazy about seeking after their treasure, then chances are they would not reap the benefits of those willing to work hard. They sometimes had to dig deep into a mountain to find it. Exploring the Colorado Rockies, I ran across many a hole that miners of old had dug apparently yielding nothing. But if they were determined and had a believing attitude, more than likely their efforts would reap results. It was only the determined miner who received his just reward for his labor. Likewise, those that actively seek after truth will find it.

However, there were hard workers that were not successful. Maybe it was because they didn't have a positive attitude, but instead thought negatively. They worked their tails off, but didn't believe their efforts would be successful in finding the gold they were seeking. A negative attitude can affect the outcome of our efforts usually for the worse, unless we change it for the better.

We can conclude that we must seek the truth with earnest desire having hope rooted in faith that we will find that which we are searching for. Jesus spoke in parables so we might search the Scriptures for revelation. Having an earnest desire to know truth through His Spirit, He will reveal truth to us.

A perfect example of a parable that Jesus told the multitudes was of the sower and was recorded in the book of Mathew (13:1-9):

On that day Jesus went out of the house, and was sitting by the sea. And great multitudes gathered to Him, so that He got into a boat and sat down, and the whole multitude was standing on the beach. And He spoke many things to them in parables, saying, "Behold, the sower went out to sow; and as he sowed, some seeds fell beside the road, and the birds came and ate them up. And others fell upon the rocky places, where they did not have much soil; and immediately they sprang up, because they had no depth of soil. But when the sun had risen, they were scorched; and because they had no root, they withered away. And others fell among the thorns, and the thorns came up and choked them out. And others fell on the good soil, and yielded a crop, some a hundredfold, some sixty, and some thirty.

He who has ears, let him hear.

This would be difficult for most of us to understand without an explanation and could cause controversy. However, in this particular parable Jesus gave His disciples understanding because they asked Him. Just as they asked to understand His story, I believe if we ask Jesus for understanding on a particular Scripture, He will answer our prayer by His Spirit guiding us to the answers we seek.

Here are the words of Jesus explaining the meaning of the parable of the sower found in Mathew 13:18-23:

Hear then the parable of the sower,

When anyone hears the word of the kingdom, and does not understand it, the evil one comes and snatches away what has been sown in his heart. This is the one on whom the seed was sown beside the road.

And the one on whom seed was sown on the rocky places, this the man who hears the word, and immediately receives it with joy; yet he has no firm root in himself, but is only temporary, and when affliction or persecution arises because of the word, immediately he falls away.

And the one on whom seed was sown among the thorns, this is the man who hears the word, and the worry of the world, and the deceitfulness of riches choke

> *the word, and it becomes unfruitful.*
>
> *And the one on whom seed was sown on the good soil, this is the man who hears the word and understands it; who indeed bears fruit, and brings forth, some a hundredfold, some sixty, and some thirty.*

We see that the "seed" is the Word of God as we read Luke 8:11, *"Now the parable is this: the seed is the Word of God."* Which of the four "seed" categories will you be in?

- The one who hears and does not understand.
- The one who has no firm root in himself.
- The one who has the thorns choke out the word.
- Or the one who is in good soil.

THE WORD BECAME FLESH

Jesus is the Word. The Word was with God and the Word was God. He is the first-born of all creation (Colossians 1:15). He is the Light. All things that came into being came into being through Him. He became flesh and dwelt among us. In the book of John 1:1-14 we can read the precious words that give evidence that Jesus is the Word and was God incarnate:

> *In the beginning was the Word, and the Word was with God, and the Word was God. He was in the beginning with God. All things came into being by Him, and apart from Him nothing came into being that has come into being. In Him was life, and the life was the Light of men. And the Light shines in the darkness, and the darkness*

did not comprehend it. There came a man, sent from God, whose name was John. He came for a witness, that he might bear witness of the Light, that all might believe through Him. He was not the Light, but came that he might bear witness of the Light. There was the true Light which, coming into the world, enlightens every man. He was in the world, and the world was made through Him, and the world did not know Him. He came to His own, and those who were His own did not receive Him. But as many as received Him, to them He gave the right to become children of God, even to those who believe in His name, who were born not of blood, nor of the will of the flesh, nor of the will of man, but of God. And the Word became flesh, and dwelt among us, and we beheld His glory, glory as of the only begotten from the Father, full of grace and truth.

"The Word became flesh and dwelt among us." How incredible is this that God, the Creator of the universe, took on flesh and was tempted as we are. Yet He remained pure and sinless, taking the sin of the world, our sin, to the cross. He did this in order to pour forth His grace (unearned favor) of forgiveness on all who believe…even you.

This forgiveness was made retroactive from Adam to all who had lived righteous lives and heard His voice, and to all those who have come after Him to the end of the age. He has risen and is now seated at the right hand of God having all power and authority both in Heaven and on earth.

I pray that the eyes of your heart may be enlightened, so that you may know what is the hope of His calling, what are the riches of the glory of His inheritance in the saints, and what is the surpassing greatness of His power toward us who believe. These are in accordance with the working of the strength of His might, which He brought about in Christ, when He raised Him from the dead, and seated Him at His right hand in the heavenly places, far above all rule and authority and power and dominion, and every name that is named, not only in this age, but also in the one to come. And He put all things in subjection under His feet, and gave Him as head over all things to the church, which is His body, the fullness of Him who fills all in all.

This power and authority is made available to us if we only believe in Him. How magnificent is this! How amazing is this! He loved us so much that He would die a horrible death and actually experience separation from God because of all the sin of the ages yet, He was sinless. He did this in order to give us hope and freedom from the bondage of sin and give us eternal life in His love, once for all. If only we believe in Him and accept His sacrifice for all our indiscretions, our names will be written in the book of life.

The word of God brings about righteousness and salvation through Jesus Christ. Hear the words that express this in Romans 10:8-11:

"...THE WORD IS NEAR YOU, IN YOUR MOUTH AND IN

> YOUR HEART."—*that is, the word of faith which we are preaching, that if you confess with your mouth Jesus as Lord, and believe in your heart that God raised Him from the dead, you shall be saved; for with the heart man believes, resulting in righteousness, and with the mouth he confesses, resulting in salvation. For the Scripture says, "WHOEVER BELIEVES IN HIM WILL NOT BE DISAPPOINTED."*

Doesn't that make you want to know the truth? Doesn't that make you want to read His word and come to know the Word and understand the wisdom and knowledge He placed there for us? Doesn't that motivate you, to want to learn more about Him and the message He eagerly wants to give us? His word has survived thousands of years and cannot be destroyed. His word expresses the very nature of the Word, Jesus.

MY EXPERIENCE READING THE WORD

In 1993 my wife to be bought me a Bible, and I made the decision to read it from cover to cover. That journey took me three years, but during that time I immersed myself so deeply in God's word that it transformed my life. As my understanding of God and His word grew, my perspective on the world changed and I began to develop spiritual discernment. Now I'm able to see through the deception, lies and misleading information we are subjected to each day more clearly.

As a result, I have come to realize that the Bible is the "Living and Enduring Word of God" (1 Peter 1:23), and this could only have been possible by His Holy Spirit. We have been "born again" through the living and abiding word of God. It continues to feed my spirit with increased faith, hope, wisdom, understanding, knowledge, discernment, grace, and love. It has given me a fresh new perspective on life with a mind set based on foundational truth; not of the world, which is deception and brings about death, but instead on one that leads to life—eternal life.

However, reading the Scriptures further opened the eyes of my heart and as a result I gained increased knowledge that rang true to the core of my being. It's like when things go right everything falls into place. Take for instance when you graduate from high school or college. You have a sense of accomplishment and of being filled with knowledge better prepared to face the world.

I'm also better able to see myself, as others do, and being more focused on my own behavior has given me a new life perspective. For me, reading God's Word cover to cover was a spiritual awakening.

THE ENEMY WILL ATTEMPT TO STOP YOU

When our heart is condemning us, we must ask for forgiveness with a sincere repentant heart. Otherwise, it may impede our ability to understand His word. However, we must not allow the enemy to whisper in our ears, "you are not worthy," or "you don't deserve forgiveness," or "your sins are too great to receive forgiveness." It may help to know that we all make mistakes and fall short; we are all sinners. As it is written in

Romans 3:23, "*...for all have sinned and fall short of the glory of God.*"

We fall victim far too often to the condemning voice of the enemy, which many times keeps us in the bondage of sin. Even those of us who have sincerely repented can fall victim to this deceptive ploy of Satan (the enemy) because we allow him to convince us we have not been forgiven. Therefore, we must believe, in faith, we are forgiven. When we do so, an incredible thing will take place. God's forgiving grace will free our heart and mind from the bondage of sin, and the Holy Spirit will fill our hearts with understanding.

Again, remember that the enemy doesn't want you to learn the truth. He will keep you from this with all his might. He'll use the strongholds in your mind that he's established throughout your lifetime to keep you from knowing forgiveness. You'll hear his lying words and think of them as your own. He is the master of deception and the author of deceitfulness. As it was written in Genesis 3:1, "*Now the serpent was more crafty than any beast of the field.*" And later in verse 13, Eve stated, "*The serpent deceived me, and I ate.*" But also know that the weakness of God is stronger then the greatest strength of the enemy, so do not fear.

In the book of 1 John (4:1-4), we see this truth made evident. We are also told to test the spirits:

> *Beloved, do not believe every spirit, but test the spirits to see whether they are from God; because many false prophets have gone out into the world. By this you know*

the Spirit of God: every spirit that confesses that Jesus Christ has come in the flesh is from God; and every spirit that does not confess Jesus is not from God; and this is the spirit of the antichrist, of which you have heard that it is coming, and now it is already in the world. You are from God, little children, and have overcome them; because greater is He who is in you than he who is in the world.

From the start, earth was made the battle ground. It is Satan's only hope of bargaining with God. If he can trick enough of us, he has hope that God will have to honor his disobedience and arrogance with some plea bargaining. But that is not going to happen because we will all learn the truth and have the opportunity to choose the One and only true God as we exercise our free will.

Read the Word; don't Procrastinate

There is no time like the present to start reading the most important book you will ever read. The Bible, the Word of the living God contains absolute Truth and answers to all of your questions. Read it and let it transform your heart and mind and you will come to know the nature of God. God and His Word is from everlasting to everlasting (Psalm 90:2).

Smith Wigglesworth was a man of extraordinary faith. He was born in 1859 and died in 1947. Fortunately, many of his words and his life experiences have been recorded and published in a book named "Smith Wigglesworth –

Devotional." In Smiths' book, he mentions an unnamed man having once said the following, about the written Word of God:

> "Never compare this Book [the Bible] with other books. Comparisons are dangerous. Never think or say that this Book contains the Word of God. It is the Word of God. It is supernatural in origin, eternal in duration, inexpressible in value, infinite in scope, regenerative in power, infallible in authority, universal in interest, personal in application, inspired in totality. Read it through. Write it down. Pray it in. Work it out. Then pass it on."

Yes, you will find God revealed within the covers of the Bible, but you will also find eternal life through the innocent blood of Jesus, the sinless one. You will find grace abounding. You will find faith beyond understanding. You will find discernment. You will find Love. You will find peace of mind and a heart filled with God's Holy Spirit. Don't expect this to happen overnight. It could, but it may take many weeks, years or even a lifetime, but stay the course and victory will be yours.

When you make the choice to start reading the Scriptures, start at the beginning--in Genesis. Don't expect it all to make sense. In fact, much of it won't. You will read about injustice and, quite frankly, things that may puzzle you or even disturb or anger you. But keep an open mind before you throw the baby out with the bath water. Stay the course and don't expect it to capture your full attention as a good mystery novel.

Instead, read it with the intention of knowing the truth about God and His Son, Jesus. Allow Him to reveal Himself through His Word and know that increased measures of faith come from hearing, and hearing from the Word of God (Romans 10:17).

However, don't be discouraged if while reading His word you don't understand a particular passage. Truth will come, but it may not be revealed all at once. Just as a newborn baby is fed milk at first, so will we, and as we mature, we will be given solid food. Even today, as I continue to read the Word, more is revealed each time I revisit the same passages. Let's read the words recorded in 1 Corinthians 3:1-3 for a better understanding:

And I, brethren, could not speak to you as to spiritual men, but as to men of flesh, as to babes in Christ. I gave you milk to drink, not solid food; for you were not yet able to receive it. Indeed, even now you are not yet able, for you are still fleshly. For since there is jealousy and strife among you, are you not fleshly, and are you not walking like mere men?

Let us be encouraged by the verses in 1 John 3:19-22 and allow our faith to grow by His Word:

We shall know by this that we are of the truth, and shall assure our heart before Him, in whatever our heart does not condemn us, we have confidence before God; and whatever we ask we receive from Him,"

Get our hearts right and, *"what ever we ask we receive from Him."* This has always been a faith builder for me; if I go to the Lord with a sincere heart, I will be heard and will be gifted with whatever I ask of Him. Therefore, if I ask for understanding of His word, I will be given truth in abundance.

Again, we are told, in the Scriptures, that the word of God is tested (Proverbs 30:5), it stands forever (Isaiah 40:8), and that man shall not live on bread alone, but on every word that proceeds out of the mouth of God (Mathew 4:4). It is from everlasting to everlasting (Psalms 90:2). Read it through, write it down, pray it in, work it out and pass it on.

Chapter 2

A FATHER TO US ALL

Ostensibly, each of us had a father procreate us by the physical relationship he had with our mothers. Of course, some of us never knew our father for one reason or another, or had little contact with him due to a divorce or other circumstances. Yet the yearning desire for a good father relationship is there whether you want to accept it or not.

You may have had love for him even if you were mistreated by him or even if you never knew him. That love may have been substituted by a burning hatred for him, but deep inside, the love is still there hidden away. It may be easier to hate rather than to love for a hope that was constantly dashed.

Regardless of the current relationship you have with your biological father, the fact remains that you do have one even if he was never part of your life. And for those of us whose father is no longer living, there may be an open pit that needs to be filled. The father relationship we have, or the lack thereof, affects our interactions with others and relationships and can during the course of our entire life.

Chapter 2

My Parents and Their Parents

My father was born in 1914 and never knew his own father. His mother, my grandmother, was six months pregnant with him at the time of his father's death. He was the last of eight children whom my grandmother raised by herself having never remarried. The father figure in my dad's life was his only brother, Frank. I'll never forget how my father wept when his brother died. The pain and agony he suffered was only understood when I lost him in 2002.

My mother had a quite different experience. She was one of four daughters. At age 11 she had a good life with her family. Her father, being a coal miner in Pennsylvania, worked hard, put in long hours and came home dirty every night. But one day he left for work and never came home. They don't know whether he chose to leave his family or that he had been killed, but the fact is no one ever saw him again. The hurt and confusion that replaced the love she had for her father was with her to the grave.

That was only the start of a very difficult life for my mother and her siblings. Her mother, my grandmother, had to find work. The work she had kept her from home most of the time as she worked very long hours to make ends meet. This, of course, caused her daughters to fend for themselves leaving them vulnerable to the difficulties during the great depression. When a drunk sex offender was caught breaking into their studio apartment, my grandmother had to give up her children to foster care. My mother was split up from her sisters and moved from home to home. It was a miserable existence for all the girls, since she had come to know and appreciate the comfort of a family unit that was now lost forever.

God the Father is Love

I don't think any of us will truly know how the relationship with our respective fathers have shaped and formed who we are today unless we come to know the Father of us all. I don't think we can forgive our own fathers for the pains of our youth unless we come to know our heavenly Father. Even if we had a perfectly good relationship with our earthly father having no youthful pains, will we be able to fully understand love itself unless we come to know our heavenly Father.

I'm not saying we couldn't have come to know love by any other way. That would be silly! For all love is from God (1 John 4:7). Instead, what I'm trying to say is that none of us may ever know the depths of love our heavenly Father has for us.

God is the author of love; He is Love (1 John 4:8). He has more Love for us than we can possibly comprehend (Romans 8:38-39). He will comfort us when we come to Him. He will protect us if we will only let Him. He will teach us and reveal the secrets of heaven to us. He will hold us in His hands and clear the path for us when we walk with Him. If we trust in Him, He is faithful. He is patient for us to come to Him. He loves us even when we don't love Him. He will discipline us (Hebrews 12:5-11) when we need it, but forgive us when we ask Him. He will give us increased measures of faith when we ask of Him in sincerity and lean on Him for support.

He is the perfect Father, having no faults, having pure unconditional love for us (Ephesians 2:4-8). He knew us and chose us in Him before the foundation of the world. We see this is true in Ephesians 1:4-5:

> ...just as He chose us in Him before the foundation of the world, that we should be holy and blameless before Him. In love He predestined us to adoption as sons through Jesus Christ to Himself, according to the kind intention of His will.

He knew us before we were formed in the womb as we read in Jeremiah 1:5, *"Before I formed you in the womb I knew you, And before you were born I consecrated you…"* He loves us so much that He gave us free will to make our own decisions, even if that means rejecting Him. However, there are consequences for the decisions we make as He will never force us to turn toward Him, nor will He stop us from turning away.

When I was 17 years old, I left my father's home. I was truly on my own. My father was no longer watching over my shoulder and I had free will to go where I wanted, do what I chose to do and when I chose to do it. However, I had his teachings and the morale compass he planted in my heart. That of course helped guide me in the daily decisions I had to make, but not always did I chose to follow my good conscience. I had free will to turn away from his good teachings and do as I pleased, but there were consequences to those detours.

Life Without Love

Can you think of what life would be like without goodness and love in the world? If you removed all goodness and love from the world, what would be left behind? It doesn't take a rocket scientist to understand that everything not good would be left behind; things like hate, greed, pride, deceit, darkness and so much more.

Yes, darkness because God is Love (1 John 4:8, 16) and the Light of the world. Remove God from the world and we would be left in darkness. In John 1:4 it is written, *"In Him was life, and life was the Light of men. And the Light shines in the darkness, and the darkness did not comprehend it,"* In John 8:12, *"Again, therefore Jesus spoke to them, saying, 'I am the Light of the world; he who follows Me shall not walk in the darkness, but shall have the Light of life.'"* And in John 9:5, *"While I am in the world, I am the Light of the world."* Once again in John 12:46, *"I have come as Light into the world, that everyone who believes in Me, may not remain in the darkness."*

Let's take it a step further. If you remove love from the world, then life would be hell on earth. Know that hell is reserved for those who reject God by their own free will. It will be a choice that all will make in time, even to our dying breath, so make it well.

If God is For Us, Who Can Be Against Us?

God the Father wants all of us to turn to Him, but again He will not force us. If that doesn't prove His love for us, than nothing I can tell you will change your mind.

When I was just a young boy, something happened at home that made me decide to run away. I brought great pain to my mother's heart because I was her child; she birthed me in pain. The love of parents for their children runs deep, so I can only imagine how our heavenly Father would feel if we chose to turn away from Him.

Just as our parents would come looking for us if we ran away from home, so the Father comes looking for us. He sends people into our lives that will point us back to Him; or He places a book in our hands; or He will allow something to come into our lives, a trial perhaps, or a challenge, or even a tragedy.

I would urge you not to turn away from Him. Instead, turn to Him and He will help you through your trial, challenge or the tragedy. Seek His help and He will comfort and love you. He Himself is not capable of performing bad things because there is only goodness and love in Him. However, He may allow the enemy to cause bad things to happen to us (refer to Job chapter 2). We might in our ignorance blame Him for those unfortunate events. But even the bad things that happen in our lives ultimately turn out for our good although we may not see it at the time.

In Romans 8:28 it is written, *"And we know that God causes all things to work together for good to those who love God, to those who are called according to His purpose."*

In 1996, I was blessed with a management job that I thought would last the rest of my adult life, until retirement. Almost my entire working life I had been in business for myself and this was to be a time when I could rest a little from the hard work of running my own business. What I thought was intended to provide me with lasting security ended up being the job from hell.

There was back stabbing and the politics were something that I was not accustomed to dealing with. It was an eye opening experience in the world of corporate America. During that year, my stomach had knotted up so tightly that pain emanated throughout my entire abdominal area.

By the end of the first year, things hadn't gotten any better, and I knew that I wouldn't make it until I retired. I prayed to the Father with all my heart to help me, and He did so, being faithful like He is. Except the help I got from Him wasn't quite what I had expected. I was called into my boss's office one Friday afternoon and told that I would offer my resignation and sign a letter that had been prepared for me or I would be fired on the spot.

I'd never been fired from a job in my entire life. My earthly father had taught me well how to work hard, and I learned a set of ethics found rarely in today's working world.

This couldn't be happening to me, this wasn't possible, I thought. For six months afterwards, I was depressed to the point of welcoming death. For me, there was nothing more painful that I had ever experienced before this rejection. But like the Scriptures teach us, all things no matter how bad they appear, ultimately turn out for good. Although I knew this to be true, it was so very difficult to believe it at the time.

If God is for us, who can be against us? This Scripture

helped me get through that horrible experience when the Holy Spirit directed me to the book of Romans 8:31-32:

What then shall we say to these things: If God is for us, who can be against us? He who did not spare His own Son, but delivered Him up for us all, how will He not also with Him freely give us all things.

No Pain, No Gain!

I didn't see the blessings that were in my future at the time, but God the Father restored the wealth I lost due to a divorce some years earlier. The people I met while at the job had been instrumental in getting me contracts I wouldn't have had otherwise. They saw the injustice that was done and wanted to help. With all the pain associated with it, who would have known why I had to go through that experience? But in the end, I received a blessing far outweighing the pain I suffered.

God the Father used the pain and agony of the experience (trial) to temper and grow me spiritually. Take for instance the making of a beautiful Samurai sword. The sword first has to go through the fire many times before it is fashioned in the likeness of a sword. It has to be heated red hot, hammered and folded and reheated. Then it must be hammered and folded again and again with a heavy hammer many times. Finally, it must be tempered before it becomes sharp enough to slice through bone with ease. This is just like us in the formation of our character and in growing in the Spirit of the Father. The process is not always cheerful, but the result is magnificent.

Our heavenly Father is the potter and we are His clay. His hands are on us molding and shaping us into the beautiful instrument of His desire. Would it hurt to be shaped and changed into a different shape? Of course it would. But as He fashions us in His likeness, we become something of beauty and useful to Him.

You've heard the saying, when referring to exercise, "No pain, no gain." If you want a body of muscle, you have to do the hard work and that will hurt. Your body will ache, but the result will be noticeably good. You will even feel better about yourself having a sense of accomplishment and worth, not to mention feeling physically better. It's no different than the discipline of a parent; it may hurt, but you will gain from it.

What earthly father doesn't discipline his son or daughter? Our heavenly Father disciplines us as well. But know that just as a loving parent disciplines, so does our heavenly Father. Paul explains this in Hebrews 12:5-11 (caps represent Old Testament quotes: see Job 5:17-18 and Proverbs 3:11-12):

> *…and you have forgotten the exhortation which is addressed to you as sons, "MY SON, DO NOT REGARD THE DISCIPLINE OF THE LORD, NOR FAINT WHEN YOU ARE REPROVED BY HIM, FOR THOSE WHOM THE LORD LOVES HE DISCIPLINES, AND HE SCOURGES EVERY SON WHOM HE RECEIVES." It is for discipline that you endure; God deals with you as with sons; for what son is there whom his father does not discipline? But if you are without discipline, of which all have become partakers, then you*

> *are illegitimate children and not sons. Furthermore, we had earthly fathers to discipline us, and we respected them; shall we not much rather be subject to the Father of spirits and live? For they disciplined us for a short time as seemed best to them, but He disciplines us for our good, that we may share His holiness. All discipline for the moment seems not to be joyful, but sorrowful; yet to those who have been trained by it, afterwards it yields the peaceful fruit of righteousness.*

Trials beget character; growth and the pain from those trials begets the maturity of your soul. We are a diamond in the rough or a lump of clay that God the Father will fashion into a thing of beauty that will radiate for others to see, if we will only allow Him. Trust Him with your life and surrender your will to Him, today, that He may fashion you into all that He wants you to be.

You see, even Jesus, who was beaten beyond recognition and who was put to death on a cross on our behalf, experienced something more horrible than any of us have or will ever go through. And I might add, it was not for anything He had done wrong, for He was wholly innocent. Despite dying a horrible death and being separated from the Father's love because of our sin, He was raised up on the third day and now sits in glory on the Fathers right side. All things have been put into subjection to His authority, both in heaven and on the earth.

Trusting in our Heavenly Father

He is our Father and He loves us more than words can describe. Our very hairs are numbered as is written in Mathew 10:30, *"but the very hairs of your head are all numbered."* He knows everything about you and He still loves you. He is patiently waiting at the door of your heart. Let Him in and He'll love you and fill the void in your life with His love.

He wants to be a Father to us so much, and His words confirm this in the book of 2 Corinthians (6:18), *"'And I will be a father to you, and you shall be sons and daughters to Me', says the Lord Almighty."*

While our heavenly Father loves us, He also wants us to do His will. When we were young, we bent to our earthly fathers will. But as adults, not only does God want us to relinquish the free will He gave us, but it requires that we trust in Him as well. Let me ask a couple of questions. Do you think God knows what is best for you? Do you think He knows what you need to learn while going through this life experience in preparation for eternity? These may be difficult questions to answer, but it is where "the rubber meets the road," if we are going to trust in Him.

We read all through the New Testament that Jesus Himself trusted in the Father, totally. He did nothing on earth that wasn't His Father's will. He surrendered His own will in obedience to the Father. For us, it may be difficult to take that first step in relinquishing our will in order to do His will. If we learn to trust in Him, as Jesus did, we will be blessed in abundance more than we can ask or think. It doesn't necessarily mean there still won't be life challenges to get through, because more likely there will be.

Furthermore, we learn that not even the words that were uttered from Jesus' mouth were His own, but were the words of the Father. That is total submission to the Father's will. It is dying to one's self totally. We read the words that He spoke to the Jews and were recorded in the book of John (12:49-50):

> *For I did not speak on My own initiative, but the Father Himself who sent Me has given Me commandment, what to say and what to speak. And I know that His commandment is eternal life; therefore the things I speak, I speak just as the Father has told Me.*

Lift up Our Prayers to the Father

Jesus was the example for us to follow. He even told us how to pray as we read in Mathew 6:9-13:

> *But you, when you pray, go into your inner room, and when you have shut your door, pray to your Father who is in secret, and your Father who sees in secret will repay you. And when you are praying, do not use meaningless repetition, as the Gentiles do, for they suppose that they will be heard for their many words. Therefore do not be like them; for your Father knows what you need, before you ask Him. Pray, then, in this way:*
> *Our Father who art in heaven,*
> *Hallowed be Thy name.*
> *Thy kingdom come.*

Thy will be done,
On earth as it is in heaven.
Give us this day our daily bread.
And forgive us our debts, as we also have forgiven our debtors.
And do not lead us into temptation, but deliver us from evil.
(For Thine is the kingdom, and the power, and the glory, forever. Amen.)

This doesn't mean that this is the only way to pray to the Father. Jesus is simply pointing out the importance of how we pray in that we:

1. praise the Father recognizing His supremacy;
2. are in agreement and aspire to do His will;
3. depend on Him to provide all things for us;
4. ask for His forgiveness when we make sinful mistakes;
5. forgive others who sin against us;
6. depend on Him to protect us from the wiles of the enemy.

God the Father wants us to depend on Him when we lift up our needs to Him because He understands our needs before we ask. Let's read the words for ourselves in Romans 8:26-27, that His Spirit will intercede for us when we are in need:

And in the same way the Spirit also helps our weakness; for we do not know how to pray as we should, but the

> *Spirit Himself intercedes for us with groaning too deep for words; and He who searches the hearts know what the mind of the Spirit is, because He intercedes for the saints according to the will of God.*

The Holy Spirit will intercede for us when we pray. When we trust in the Father for all things, He will make our paths straight.

The Father's Gift to Us is Realized Through Jesus

The Father wants to bless us beyond our wildest dreams, even though we fall short being the sinners we are. If you doubt this, then you are in denial being influenced by the lies of the enemy. One example that our heavenly Father wants to bless us can be found in the book of Mathew (7:11); again the words of Jesus:

> *If you then, being evil, know how to give good gifts to your children, how much more shall your Father who is in heaven give what is good to those who ask Him!*

Another such example can be found in the book of Romans 8:32, *"He who did not spare His own Son, but delivered Him over for us all, how will He not also with Him freely give us all things?"* Did you catch that? With Jesus, the Father will freely give us all things. We see as we continue to read in Romans, that it is Jesus who intercedes for us to the Father as described in verses 33-39:

> *Who will bring a charge against God's elect? God is the one who justifies; who is the one who condemns? Christ Jesus is He who died, yes, rather who was raised, who is at the right hand of God, who also intercedes for us. Who shall separate us from the love of Christ: Shall tribulation, or distress, or persecution, or famine, or nakedness, or peril, or sword? Just as it is written, "FOR THY SAKE WE ARE BEING PUT TO DEATH ALL DAY LONG; WE WERE CONSIDERED AS SHEEP TO BE SLAUGHTERED." But in all these things we overwhelmingly conquer through Him who loved us. For I am convinced that neither death, nor life, nor angels, nor principalities, nor things present, nor things to come, nor powers, nor height, nor depth, nor any other created things, shall be able to separate us from the love of God, which is in Christ Jesus our Lord.*

We are told that the way to the Father is through Jesus Christ. The Father is in Jesus and Jesus is in the Father and we are in Him. If you want to know the love of the Father you need only pray to the Father through Jesus. Speak your prayer to the Father in the name of Jesus. Let's read the words that Jesus spoke to His disciples in the book of John (14:1-20):

> *Let not your heart be troubled; believe in God, believe also in Me. In My Father's house are many dwelling places; if it were not so, I would have told you; for I go to prepare a place for you. And if I go and prepare a place for you, I will come again, and receive you to Myself;*

that where I am, there you may be also. And you know the way where I am going.

Thomas said to Him, "Lord, we do not know where You are going, how do we know the way?" Jesus said to him, "I am the way, and the truth, and the life; no one comes to the Father, but through Me. If you had known Me, you would have known My Father also; from now on you know Him, and have seen Him."

Philip said to Him, "Lord, show us the Father, and it is enough for us." Jesus said to him, "Have I been so long with you and yet you have not come to know Me, Philip? He who has seen Me has seen the Father; how do you say, 'Show us the Father?' Do you not believe that I am in the Father, and the Father is in Me? The words that I say to you I do not speak on My own initiative, but the Father abiding in Me does His works. Believe Me that I am in the Father, and the Father in Me; otherwise believe on account of the works themselves. Truly, truly, I say to you, he who believes in Me, the works that I do shall he do also; and greater words than these shall he do; because I go to the Father. And whatever you ask in My name, that will I do, that the Father may be glorified in the Son. If you ask Me anything in My name, I will do it. If you love Me, you will keep My commandments. And I will ask the Father, and He will give you another Helper, that He may be with you forever; that is the Spirit of truth, whom the world cannot receive, because it does not behold Him or know Him, but you know

Him because He abides with you, and will be in you. I will not leave you as orphans; I will come to you. After a little while the world will behold Me no more; but you will behold Me; because I live, you shall live also. In that day you shall know that I am in My Father, and you in Me, and I in you."

Jesus said, *"Just as the Father has loved Me, I have also loved you; abide in My love. If you keep My commandments, you will abide in My love; just as I have kept My Father's commandments, and abide in His love."*

The ultimate love is laying down your life for a brother. That act of love Jesus demonstrated for all of us is evidenced by His sacrifice on the cross. It was our sins, transgressions and shame that were nailed to the cross.

Let us not forget that Jesus was God incarnate, creator of everything (John chapter 1). His deity is recorded all through the Scriptures. He came from heaven and took on flesh on our behalf through the love He has for us in order that we have the means to attain eternal life through Him. He is one person of the Triune God: Father, Son, and the Holy Spirit. It is a mystery, but Scriptures give us clear insight about this both in the Old and New Testaments.

If there is emptiness in your heart for the father you never knew, or if you want to be healed in your earthly father relationship, start by coming to know our heavenly Father through Jesus. Trust in Him and He will heal all your hurts and all your wounds. He will fill your heart with His loving Spirit. Come to Him, He is waiting to sooth your being.

Chapter 3

JESUS WALKED AMONG US

Jesus walked the earth two thousand years ago and we are still debating His life today. The few recorded words He spoke during the short time He walked among us has had an impact on the lives of all who have read them in one way or another. No man has caused more controversy than He. No man has touched the hearts of more people than He. No man has had a more positive life giving message throughout the centuries to us all than He. And the Love example He demonstrated then, continues today and will until His second coming.

In an earlier chapter, we established that the Bible was breathed into existence by God, written by men, but inspired by God. In this chapter, we will explore what is said about Jesus within the depths of the Scriptures. Specifically, we will be focusing on verses from both the Old Testament and the New Testaments giving insight into prophesy; His deity and pre-existence; His person in the trinity; His priesthood, ancestry and birth; and His divine purpose—our salvation.

Prophesy

We find many prophecies written of Jesus throughout the Old Testament some fifteen hundred years before His birth. The prophecies were written about His ancestry, deity, birth, death and suffering, character, ministry, resurrection and even His ascension into heaven. There are literally hundreds of predictions about Jesus, the Messiah, and all have been fulfilled and recorded in the New Testament, with the exception of His future second coming. Jesus is the only man in the history of the world who has had detailed prophetic Scriptures written by more than a score of prophets over the centuries and have all been accurately realized by His recorded life. One way to describe the complexity and incredible odds of this happening is done by Canon Dyson Hague:

> Who could draw a picture of a man not yet born? Surely God, and God alone. Nobody knew over 500 years ago that Shakespeare was going to be born; or over 250 years ago that Napoleon was to be born. Yet here in the Bible we have the most striking and unmistakable likeness of a Man portrayed, not by one, but by twenty or twenty-five artists, none of whom had ever seen the Man they were painting.

Think about that for a moment—all prophesy of Jesus has been fulfilled with the exception of His second coming. The prophets who were led by the Holy Spirit, accurately expressed these divine visions with specific events and specific accomplishments, before He was born, and yet they were ALL fulfilled during Jesus' lifetime.

In Lockyer's *All the Messianic Prophesies of the Bible*, he further demonstrates the incredible odds of this occurring. He also quotes from Pierson's *God's Living Oracles*, giving us a further appreciation of what the odds might be of this occurring:

> The literal fulfillment of a prophecy is the seal of its divine origin. Prophecies of centuries concerning the final sufferings of Christ were fulfilled during the twenty-four hours leading up to His crucifixion. According to the law of compound probabilities, the conservative chance that they all happened together by accident is one in 537 million. However, in Pierson's *God's Living Oracles*, this renowned Bible scholar says that there are:
>
>> ...over 300 predictions about the Messiah to be found in the Old Testament. According to the law of compound probability, the chance of their coming true is represented by a fraction whose numerator is one, and the denominator eighty-four followed by nearly one-hundred ciphers. One might almost as well expect by accident to dip up any one particular drop out of the ocean as to expect so many prophetic rays to converge by chance upon one man, in one place, at one time. God has put especially upon these

prophecies as to His Son the *stamp of absolute verity and indisputable certainty*, so that we may know whom we have believed. Mistakes in so solemn a matter are fatal and God meant that none should be possible.

HIS DEITY AND PRE-EXISTENCE

His deity has been questioned, and many have wrongly portrayed him as a sinner and a mere man. But as we explore the Scriptures, we will find that He is much more than just a mere man who lived His life and died. There were 500 men and women who witnessed Him after His resurrection and watched Him ascend into heaven. He is the living God who took on flesh and resisted temptation to the point of sweating blood and remained pure and sinless to the end of His earthly life.

The Scripture in the book of John must be restated, because it is so clearly written. It, among other Scriptures, gives proof of the deity of our Lord Jesus Christ. These powerful words can be found in John 1:1-14:

> *In the beginning was the Word, and the Word was with God, and the Word was God. He was in the beginning with God. All things came into being through Him, and apart from Him nothing came into being that has come into being. In Him was life, and the life was the Light of men. The Light shines in the darkness, and the darkness did not comprehend it.*
>
> *There came a man, sent from God, whose name was*

John. He came for a witness, that he might bear witness of the Light, that all might believe through him. He was not the Light, but came that he might bear witness of the Light. There was the true Light which, coming into the world, enlightens every man. He was in the world, and the world was made through Him, and the world did not know Him. He came to His own, and those who were His own did not receive Him. But as many as received Him, to them He gave the right to become children of God, even to those who believe in His name, who were born not of blood, nor of the will of the flesh, nor of the will of man, but of God. And the Word became flesh, and dwelt among us, and we beheld His glory, glory as of the only begotten from the Father, full of grace and truth.

Jesus is referred to as the Word, *"In the beginning was the Word, and the Word was with God, and the Word was God. He was in the beginning with God. All things came into being by Him, and apart from Him nothing came into being that has come into being."* His deity is affirmed here and gives us a glimpse into the mystery of the Trinity. He is the Word, yet the Word was with God, and the Word was God.

Jesus is also expressed as the creator of all things for, *"apart from Him nothing came into being that has come into being."*

And later in John 1:14 he expresses: *"and the Word became flesh and dwelt among us,"* clearly stating that Jesus, the deity, took on a fleshly body and walked among us. That means that

Jesus, the creator or co-creator, became God incarnate.

Also we see in Colossians 1:15-17 that His deity and pre-existence is reaffirmed:

And He is the image of the invisible God, the first-born of all creation. For by Him all things were created, both in the heavens and on earth, visible and invisible, whether thrones or dominions or rulers or authorities – all things have been created by Him and for Him. And He is before all things, and in Him all things hold together.

This leaves no doubt that Jesus was the creator or co-creator with the Father God head. It's also clear to see that He is the true Son of God, since He was the first born of all creation on a spiritual level, even before He took on flesh and lived among us. Again, it is seemingly impossible to deny His deity as the Creator of the universe.

Verse 17, however, "*…in Him all things hold together.*" is difficult to explain. If we take it for what it says, then we are in Him and He holds all things together. Jesus is apparently the body or the glue that is holding all things together. Perhaps, it means like our own bodies are held together with laminin, we are in His body.

In case you're interested, laminins are large trimeric proteins that contain an "A"-chain, a "B1"-chain, and a "B2"-chain, found in five, three and three genetic variants, respectively. The laminin molecules are named according to their chain composition. These trimeric proteins form a cross, giving a structure that can bind to other cell membrane and extracellular matrix molecules. The three shorter arms are particularly good at binding to other laminin molecules which allow them to form sheets. The long arm is capable of binding to cells, which helps anchor organized tissue cells to the membrane. They are an integral part of the structural scaffolding in almost every tissue of an organism. They are in essence what holds our bodies together—one cell to another. I am intrigued by the fact it is in the shape of a cross. Call it coincidental or call it evidence that our Creator is making available so man is without excuse (Romans 1:20).

The following is a picture of what the laminin, trimeric proteins, look like:

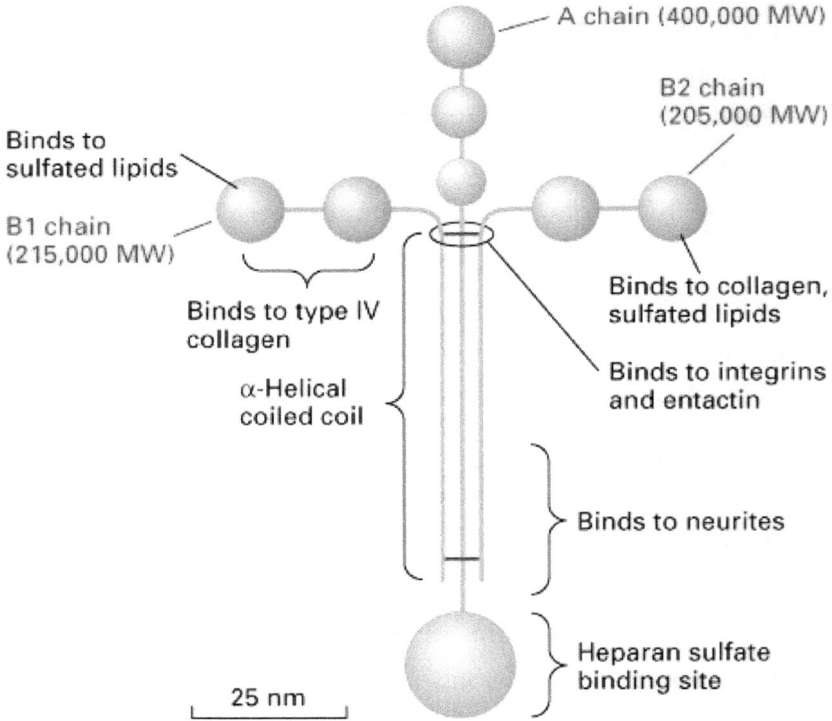

Our Jesus created all things visible and invisible; He is before all things and in Him all things are held together. This is one that I will ponder the rest of my life and search the Scriptures for insight into its meaning. This is what encourages or fires me up to read and understand the word of God, because there is so much to learn. Our scientists have only scratched the surface of knowledge of physics, quantum physics and the secrets of the universe, yet many have placed themselves above Him in their wisdom because of what they have learned or discovered.

Let's read the words found in the book of Romans stating that evidence of creation is evident to us because God made it evident to us. Those who choose to trust in man will find that their hearts have become darkened. It is also likely that those who depend on man and science for answers will become futile in their speculation. The same goes for people who place man and animals on a pedestal of importance over God. The Scripture in Romans 1:19-23 states it most clearly:

> *…because that which is known about God is evident within them; for God made it evident to them. For since the creation of the world His invisible attributes, His eternal power and divine nature, have been clearly seen, being understood through what has been made, so that they are without excuse. For even though they knew God, they did not honor Him as God, or give thanks; but they became futile in their speculations, and their foolish heart was darkened. Professing to be wise, they became*

> *fools, and exchanged the glory of the incorruptible God for an image in the form of corruptible man and of birds and four-footed animals and crawling creatures.*

Jesus is the Light of the world by His own proclamation, and was recorded in the book of John 8:12, *"Then Jesus spoke to them saying, 'I am the Light of the world; he who follows Me will not walk in the darkness, but will have the Light of life."* Jesus continues, in verse 18, to assert that God is His Father, *"I am He who testifies about Myself, and the Father who sent Me testifies about Me."* And in verse 19 Jesus spoke to the Jews, that His Father is in Him, *"So they were saying to Him, 'Where is your Father?' Jesus answered, 'You know neither Me nor My Father; if you knew Me, you would know My Father also.'"*

In John 5:18-23, Jesus proclaims that He is the Son of God to the Jews. Most likely there were Pharisees or Scribes among them, the religious leaders of the Jews, because we read they were seeking to kill Him after His assertion of Deity:

> *For this cause therefore the Jews were seeking all the more to kill Him, because He not only was breaking the Sabbath, but also was calling God His own Father, making Himself equal with God. Therefore Jesus answered and was saying to them, "Truly, truly, I say to you, the Son can do nothing of Himself, unless it is something He sees the Father doing; for whatever, the Father does, these things the Son also does in like manner. For the Father loves the Son, and shows Him all things that He Himself is doing; and the Father will*

show Him greater works than these, so that you will marvel. For, just as the Father gives them life, even so the Son also gives life to whom He wishes. For, not even the Father judges anyone, but He has given all judgment to the Son, so that all will honor the Son even as they honor the Father. He who does not honor the Son does not honor the Father who sent Him."

Jesus is the true one and only Son of God. This is a fact that cannot in all honesty be denied. The Scriptures proclaim this through multiple sources throughout recorded history.

His Person in the Trinity

Jesus is One Person in the Trinity—the Son. Our triune God is the Father, the Son, and the Holy Spirit. There is much evidence of the Trinity all through the Scriptures.

For a better understanding of this, we must look into the original Hebrew words chosen in the Scriptures. In Genesis 1:1, *"In the beginning God created the heavens and the earth."* In English we only have the singular and plural word, whereas in the original Hebrew text the singular, dual and plural are used. The Hebrew word "Elohim," pronounced el-o-hem, is plural and is also used in Genesis 1:26, *"let us make man in our own image, according to our likeness; and let them rule over the fish of the sea and over the birds of the sky and over the cattle and over all the earth,"* and is further used 2,498 times throughout the Bible. To quote Lockyer, "the term corresponds with '*let us*' (1:26), and clearly asserts the Trinity – God the Father, God the Son, and God the Spirit."

The Trinity is a mystery that is hard to wrap our arms around, but suffice it to say that the Father, the Son and the Holy Spirit are all elements of the One true God. This can only be accepted and believed in our hearts through faith and in believing the Scriptures—the word of God.

Let's read the words of Lockyer's *All about the Holy Spirit,* because I couldn't put it any better:

> The relative functions of Father, Son, and Spirit can be expressed thus: God the Father is the original source of everything (Gen. 1:1). God the Son follows in the order of revelation (John 5:22-27). God the Spirit is the channel through which the blessings of heaven reach us (Eph. 2:18). Thus, the order of divine performance is from the Father, through the Son and by the Holy Spirit.

Through Jesus, we receive from the Father by the Holy Spirit. When we pray, we lift our prayers to the Father through Jesus made possible by the Holy Spirit. It will help us understand the relationship between the Persons of the Trinity if we hear the words that Jesus spoke to His disciples and were recorded in the book of John 15:23-27 and John 16:3-15 respectively:

> *He who hates Me hates My Father also. If I had not done among them the works which no one else did, they would not have sin; but now they have both seen and hated Me and My Father as well. But they have done this in order that the word may be fulfilled that is written in*

*their Law, "*THEY HATED ME WITHOUT A CAUSE*." When the Helper comes, whom I will send to you from the Father, that is the Spirit of truth, who proceeds from the Father, He will bear witness of Me, and you will bear witness also, because you have been with Me from the beginning.*

And these things they will do, because they have not known the Father or Me. But these things I have spoken to you, that when their hour comes, you may remember that I told you of them. And these things I did not say to you at the beginning, because I was with you. But now I am going to Him who sent Me, and none of you asks Me, "Where are you going?" But because I have said these things to you, sorrow has filled your heart. But I tell you the truth, it is to your advantage that I go away; for if I do not go away, the Helper shall not come to you; but if I go, I will send Him to you. And He, when He comes, will convict the world concerning sin, and righteousness, and judgment; concerning sin, because they do not believe in Me; and concerning righteousness, because I go to the Father, and you no longer behold Me; and concerning judgment, because the ruler of this world has been judged. I have many more things to say to you, but you cannot bear them now. But when He, the Spirit of truth, comes, He will guide you into all truth; for He will not speak on His own initiative, but whatever He hears, He will speak; and He will disclose to you what is to come. He shall glorify Me; for He shall

> *take of Mine, and shall disclose it to you. All things that the Father has are Mine, therefore I said, that He takes of Mine, and will disclose it to you.*

Yes, there is evidence written in His word that leads us to understanding the mystery of the Trinity. However, it still takes faith to believe, just as with the Deity of Jesus. The good news is the Scriptures tell us that Jesus is the author and perfecter of our faith. In His word we read that the three are in agreement and can be found in the book of 1 John 5:4-8:

> *For whatever if born of God overcomes the world; and this is the victory that has overcome the world—our faith. And who is the one who overcomes the world, but he who believes that Jesus is the Son of God? This is the one who came by water and blood, Jesus Christ; not with the water only, but with the water and with the blood. And it is the Spirit who bears witness, the Spirit is the truth. For there are three that bears witness, the Spirit and the water and the blood; and the three are in agreement.*

His Priesthood

He had to be wholly innocent in order to be the sacrificial lamb, *"...once for all..."* plain and simple. This goes back to the days of old where the Law was given to Moses. In order for there to be forgiveness of sin, there had to be the shedding of blood–innocent blood once every year. And not only that, but priests were instituted by men in order to perform the ritual of forgiveness. In fact, there was appointed a high priest who would sacrifice first for himself and then for the people in the Holy of Holies. This was the inner most sanctuary of the Holy temple.

They would first tie a rope around the high priest's ankle before he would enter the Holy of Holies. That way, if his heart was not right before God and he would die in the presence of God, they could drag him back out. And again, this would only occur once a year and only the high priest could perform this ritual.

All priests were appointed by men and, of course, as in all men they would all eventually die. So there were many priests. It was all set up in ritual with rules and customs that were passed down from generation to generation. One important thing to note is that sacrifice for sin was often and continual. That's why it took place year after year. But now, because of Jesus, all this ritual became unnecessary because he died *"… once for all…"* for all our sins in the past, present and even those in our weakness we may commit in the future.

There had to be innocent blood spilled in order to cleanse us from our sin. Jesus was the innocent Lamb, the perfect Lamb without blemish, and how much more powerful is His blood sacrifice than the blood of a lamb or goat. Although there were almost constant sacrifices by all the priests, only once a year would the high priest enter the Holy of Holies for the ultimate sacrifice for himself and for all of the people. Jesus was not only the innocent lamb, but was appointed high priest in the order of Melchizedek.

Melchizedek, meaning king of righteousness, was a high priest, and he was also the king of Salem, which means king of peace. No one knows where he came from and no one knows where he went. In other words, he didn't have a beginning nor did he have an end. There is not much written about him in the Scriptures. In fact, there are only a few places where he is even mentioned in the Bible, so we don't know a whole lot about him. We do know, however, he was in fact *"…a priest of God Most High…"*. Even Abram, whose name was later changed by God to Abraham when He formed a covenant with him, paid homage to Melchizedek when he returned from war and gave him a ten per cent tithe, of all the spoils of war—the lesser (Abraham) paid the greater (Melchizedek). This also means all of the priests who came from the loins of Abraham tithed to Melchizedek as well, making him a high priest above all priests.

Paul masterfully explains this as we read Hebrews 7:1-10:

> *For this Melchizedek, king of Salem, priest of the Most High God, who met Abraham as he was returning from the slaughter of the kings and blessed him, to whom also Abraham apportioned a tenth part of all the spoils, was first of all, by translation of his name, king of righteousness, and then also king of Salem, which is king of peace. Without father, without mother, without genealogy, having neither beginning of days nor end of life, but made like the Son of God, he abides a priest perpetually.*

> *Now observe how great this man was to whom Abraham, the patriarch, gave a tenth of the choicest spoils. And to those indeed of the sons of Levi who receive the priest's office have commandment in the Law to collect a tenth from the people, that is, from their brethren, although these are descended from Abraham. But the one whose genealogy is not traced from them collected a tenth from Abraham, and blessed the one who had the promises. But without any dispute the lesser is blessed by the greater. And in this case mortal men receive tithes, but in that case one receives them, of whom it is witnessed that he lives on. And, so to speak, through Abraham even Levi, who received tithes, paid tithes, for he was still in the loins of his father when Melchizedek met him.*

This is how the blessing of Abraham by Melchizedek was recorded as we read in Genesis 14:18-20:

> *And Melchizedek king of Salem brought out bread and wine; now he was a priest of God Most High. And he blessed him and said, "Blessed be Abram of God Most High, Possessor of heaven and earth; And blessed be God Most High, Who has delivered your enemies into your hand."*

Why is all of this so important? Because David prophesied, what God spoke of His Son Jesus and we read in Psalms 110:1 and verse 4-5:

> *The Lord says to my Lord: "Sit at My right hand, Until I make Your enemies a footstool for Your feet."... The Lord has sworn and will not change His mind, "You are a priest forever, According to the order of Melchizedek." The Lord is at Your right hand...*

Jesus is therefore, *"...a priest forever, according to the order of Melchizedek...,"* having no beginning and no end, a high priest over all priests for eternity. In Hebrews 7:26-28 we read:

> *For it was fitting that we should have such a high priest, holy innocent, undefiled, separated from sinners and exalted above the heavens; who does not need daily; like those high priests, to offer up sacrifices, first for His own sins, and then for the sins of the people, because this He did **once for all** when He offered up Himself. For the Law appoints men as high priests who are weak, but the word of the oath, which came after the Law, appoints a Son, made perfect forever.*

His Nature, Words and His Ministry

In the first four books of the New Testament are the gospels of Mathew, Mark, Luke and John. As mentioned before, the literal words of Jesus were recorded in these four books. Some Bibles put His words in red ink and are referred to as the "red letter" edition. Every word was filled with meaning, for He chose His words well or didn't speak at all. He had a mission from God the Father and did His will in the few short years He walked among us. Jesus' nature was outlined throughout the New Testament, but the actual accounts of His works, His life and the words He spoke were recorded in these four Gospels as His disciples witnessed. We can read the words He spoke confirming this, as were recorded in the book of John (5:30-47):

> *I can do nothing on My own initiative. As I hear, I judge; and My judgment is just, because I do not seek My own will, but the will of Him who sent Me.*
>
> *If I alone testify about Myself, My testimony is not true. There is another who testifies of Me, and I know that the testimony which He gives about Me is true.*
>
> *You have sent to John (this is referring to John the Baptist), and he has testified to the truth. But the testimony which I receive is not from man, but I say these things so that you may be saved. He was the lamp that was burning and was shining and you were willing to rejoice for a while in his light.*
>
> *But the testimony which I have is greater than the testimony of John; for the works which the Father has given Me to accomplish—the very works that I do—testify about Me, that the Father has sent Me.*
>
> *And the Father who sent Me, He has testified of Me. You have neither heard His voice at any time nor seen His form. You do not have His word abiding in you, for you do not believe Him whom He sent.*
>
> *You search the Scriptures because you think that in them you have eternal life, it is these that testify about*

Me; and you are unwilling to come to Me so that you may have life. I do not receive glory from men; but I know you, that you do not have the love of God in yourselves. I have come in My Father's name, and you do not receive Me; if another comes in his own name, you will receive him. How can you believe, when you receive glory from one another and you do not seek the glory that is from the one and only God? Do not think that I will accuse you before the Father; the one who accuses you is Moses, in whom you have set your hope. For if you believed Moses, you would believe Me, for he wrote about Me. But if you do not believe his writings, how will you believe My words?'

Seven hundred years BC, Isaiah, the prophet, wrote a profound prophesy about Jesus. Ironically, the name Isaiah means "The Lord saves." He was one of the greatest prophets of that day. His prophesy describes the sacrifice that Jesus made for us, the unworthy. It even describes His appearance and gives us a glimpse of what Jesus was like. It would be Gods' master plan against the enemy, and death would no longer reign victorious over man. It was recorded in the book of Isaiah (53:1-12):

Who has believed our message? And to whom has the arm of the Lord been revealed? For He grew up before Him like a tender shoot, and like a root out of parched ground; He has no stately form or majesty that we should look upon Him, nor appearance that we should be attracted to Him.

He was despised and forsaken of men, a man of sorrows, and acquainted with grief; and like one from whom men hide their face, he was despised, and we did not esteem Him.

Surely our grief He Himself bore, and our sorrows He carried; yet we ourselves esteemed Him stricken, smitten of God, and afflicted. But He was pierced through for our transgressions, he was crushed for our iniquities; the chastening for our well-being fell upon Him, and by His scourging we are healed. All of us like sheep have gone astray, each of us has turned to his own way; but the Lord has caused the iniquity of us all to fall on Him.

He was oppressed and he was afflicted, yet He did not open His mouth; like a lamb that is led to slaughter, and like a sheep that is silent before its shearers, so He did not open His mouth. By oppression and judgment He was taken away; and as for His generation, who considered that He was cut off out of the land of the living, for the transgression of my people to whom the stroke was due? His grave was assigned with wicked men, yet He was with a rich man in His death, because He had done no violence, nor was there any deceit in His mouth.

But the Lord was pleased to crush Him, putting Him to grief; if He would render Himself as a guilt offering, He will see His offspring, He will prolong His days, and the good pleasure of the Lord will prosper in

His hand. As a result of the anguish of His soul, He will see it and be satisfied; by His knowledge the Righteous One, My Servant, will justify the many, as He will bear their iniquities. Therefore, I will allot Him a portion with the great, and He will divide the booty with the strong; because He poured out Himself to death, and was numbered with the transgressors; yet He Himself bore the sin of many, and interceded for the transgressors.

He bore the sin of many and He intercedes for us to the Father for our transgressions. This is the good news of the Scripture. Praise God.

His Ancestry

Now let's take a look at His ancestry as it has been recorded both in the Old Testament and in the New Testament. The lineage from Adam to Shem is recorded in the book of Genesis chapter 5 and from Shem to Abram (Abraham) in Genesis chapter 11, all representing 1,946 years. Then the lineage is recorded from Abraham to the birth of Christ in the book of Mathew, chapter 1.

The Genealogy of Jesus starts with Adam the first created man. You will note below that, when known, after the name of the father, in parenthesis, is the number of years lived before giving birth to the next recorded generation. It does not represent how long the father lived, for they lived hundreds of years before the flood came. So here it is from the beginning of creation starting, of course, with Adam:

Adam (130)
(Note: Creation starts with Adam)
Seth (105)
Enosh (90)
Kenan (70)
Mahalalel (65)
Jared (162)
Enoch (65)
(Note: Enoch never died…he was translated to God)
Methuselah (187)
(Note: Methuselah lived the longest at 969 years)
Lamech (182)
Noah (500)
(Note: the flood came and 8 people took refuge on the ark: Noah, his wife and his sons Shem, Ham, Japheth and their wives)
Shem (100)
(Note: he was the first born of triplets and survived the flood with Noah)
Arpachshad (35)
Shelah (30)
Eber (34)
Peleg (30)
Reu (32)
Serug (30)
Nahor (29)
Terah (70)
There are 14 generations from Abraham to David

Abram (Abraham)

(Note: Abraham became a father at 100 years old by divine intervention because Sarah was baron and she was past birthing years at 90 years old)

Isaac

(Note: Isaac was the only son born of Sarah to Abraham, however, he also birthed Ishmael from Hagar, Sarah's servant)

Jacob (Israel)

(Note: Jacob was the father of the 12 tribes of Israel…one son named Joseph who was sold into slavery by his brothers and then, after much pain and agony, became governor second in command of Egypt by the grace of God)

Judah

Perez

Hezron

Ram

Amminadab

Nahshon

Salmon

Boaz

Obed

Jesse

(Note: There are 14 generations from David to deportation to Babylon.)

David

(Note: As a boy he slew Goliath. He became a king and was a prophet of great faith who wrote many of the Psalms and prophesied of Jesus.)

Solomon

(Note: Solomon's mother was Bathsheba who was married to Uriah, the military commander whom David sent to the front lines…this was David's greatest sin. After Uriah's death, David married Bathsheba.)

Rehoboam

Abijah

Asa

Jehoshaphat

Joram

Uzziah

Jotham

Ahaz

Hezekiah

Manasseh

Amon

(Note: there are 14 generations from deportation to the time of Christ)

Josiah

Jeconiah

Shealtiel

Zerubbabel

Abihud

Eliakim

Azor

Zadok

Achim

Eliud
Eleazar
Matthan
Jacob
Joseph
(Note: the husband of Mary)

We can also find the lineage in Luke 3:23-38, but it differs from the account outlined in Matthew 1:1-17. Many have debated the differences. However, there is good evidence in support of the account recorded by Luke, in that it is made from a natural descent, while Mathew records the legal descent.

Lockyer, in his book, "All the Messianic Prophecies of the Bible" describes the record differences between Matthew and Luke in this way:

> The change of expression in the list is important. All through it, the Old Testament characters are linked together by the word *begat*—a term implying natural generation. But begat no longer applies, for Jesus was not begotten of natural generation, as the rest were. He was born of Mary, not of Joseph and Mary. Jesus had a human mother, but not a human father, as our next section will more fully show.
>
> Luke, in his genealogy, has the phrase 'Jesus… being (as was supposed) the son of Joseph' (3:23). Matthew speaks of Joseph as 'the son of Jacob,' but Luke describes him as 'the son of Heli.' Of course,

it was impossible for him to be the natural son of both. Luke, writing of Jesus as 'the son of man,' gives His genealogy on His mother's side through Heli who was Mary's father. Luke does not say that Heli begat Joseph, but became so (in law) to Heli on his marriage with Mary. Fausset has an enlightening comment on the seeming contradiction here:

Mary must have been of the same tribe and family as Joseph, according to the law (Num. 36:8). Isaiah implied that Messiah was the seed of David by *natural* as well as legal descent (11:1). Probably Matthan of Matthew is the Matthat of Luke, and Jacob and Heli were brothers; and Jacob's son Joseph, and Heli's daughter Mary, first cousins. Joseph as male heir of his uncle Heli, who had only one child, Mary, would marry her according to the law. Thus the genealogy of the inheritance in Matthew's list and that of *natural descent* in Luke's list would be primarily Joseph's, then Mary's also.

Further, the word 'supposed' indicates that Christ's sonship to Joseph was only a reputed, not a real one. Yet Jesus was God's extraordinary gift to Joseph through his proper wife Mary, and *the fruit of his marriage to her,* not a natural offspring of his body, but *as supernatural fruit.* Hence attention is drawn to Joseph as a 'son of David' and 'of the house and lineage of David' (Matt. 1:20; Luke 2:4; cf. Luke 1:32). Later on, Joseph and Mary are spoken of as the parents of Jesus.

Here, again, we see a fulfillment of the prophetic Scriptures. Portraying Christ, some 700 years before He was born, Isaiah could say, 'Unto us a child is born, unto us a son is given' (9:6). At Bethlehem was born the holy Child Jesus, Mary's firstborn, but as a Son he was given by God, whom Jesus claimed as His Father. He was born of a woman, but not of a woman and a man as in natural generation. As the *Child* born, we have a revelation of His humanity; as the *Son* given, His deity.

Regardless of how you look at it, it is clear that Jesus descended naturally from David through Mary and legally from David through Joseph. The Old Testament prophesies have been fulfilled.

His Virgin Birth

He took on flesh in the most humble way in a manger with farm animals. He was not born to a kingdom of luxury and fan-fare, but rather by having a most humble beginning barely noticed by anyone.

His birth was foretold throughout the Old Testament Scriptures through the prophets. However, the New Testament Scriptures, especially the accounts of Mary and Joseph, give a vivid account of how they dealt with the angelic visits that preceded the birth of Jesus.

First, we read the account of Mary being visited by the

angel Gabriel in the book of Luke (1:26-38). Now the Scripture starts out giving detail about Zacharias and Elizabeth, the future parents of John the Baptist, who were also relatives of Mary. Elizabeth is pregnant with John the Baptist six months when the passage starts, and the event was recorded as follows:

> *Now in the sixth month the angel Gabriel was sent from God to a city in Galilee, called Nazareth, to a virgin engaged to a man whose name was Joseph, of the descendants of David; and the virgin's name was Mary. And coming in, he said to her, "Hail, favored one! The Lord is with you." But she was greatly troubled at this statement, and kept pondering what kind of salutation this might be. And the angel said to her, "Do not be afraid, Mary; for you have found favor with God. And behold, you will conceive in your womb, and bear a son, and you shall name Him Jesus. He will be great, and will be called the Son of the Most High; and the Lord God will give Him the throne of His father David; and He will reign over the house of Jacob forever; and His kingdom will have no end." And Mary said to the angel, "How can this be, since I am a virgin?" And the angel answered and said to her, "The Holy Spirit will come upon you, and the power of the Most High will overshadow you; and for that reason the holy offspring shall be call the Son of God. And behold, even your relative Elizabeth has also conceived a son in her old age; and she who was called barren is now in her sixth*

> month. For nothing is impossible with God." And Mary said, "Behold, the bondslave of the Lord; be it done to me according to your word." And the angel departed from her.

In the book of Mathew (1:18-25) we read the account of Joseph after he found out that Mary was with child. His first reaction was to save Mary from disgrace and ridicule. But he was confused and troubled because he didn't understand, not totally believing how it could have come to be. Although Mary had explained everything to him, he was still very troubled and was going to send her away. It was then that Joseph had a visitation by an angel in a dream, who guided him in what he was to do:

> Now the birth of Jesus Christ was as follows. When His mother Mary had been betrothed (engaged) to Joseph, before they came together she was found to be with child by the Holy Spirit. And Joseph her husband, being a righteous man, and not wanting to disgrace her, desired to put her away secretly. But when he had considered this, behold, an angel of the Lord appeared to him in a dream, saying, "Joseph, son of David, do not be afraid to take Mary as you wife; for that which has been conceived in her is of the Holy Spirit. And she will bear a Son; and you shall call His name Jesus, for it is He who will save His people from their sins." Now all this took place that what was spoken by the Lord through the prophet (Isaiah 7:14) might be fulfilled, saying,

> "*BEHOLD, THE VIRGIN SHALL BE WITH CHILD, AND SHALL BEAR A SON, AND THEY SHALL CALL HIS NAME IMMANUEL,*" *which translated means, "GOD IS WITH US." And Joseph arose from his sleep, and did as the angel of the Lord commanded him, and took her as his wife, and kept her a virgin until she gave birth to a Son; and he called His name Jesus.*

I find it amazing that Joseph was visited by an angel in a dream, whereas with Mary, the angel Gabriel actually appeared to her in person. Typically, those who were visited by angelic figures were terrified, but not Mary. At first, she was troubled by how Gabriel had greeted her, but she was also humbled. She without doubt, however, accepted the awesome responsibility with total trust in God and in the events that would take place described to her by the angel Gabriel. She was in total submission to God's will.

What an honor for Mary to carry the creator of the universe in her womb. Can you imagine how incredible this experience might have been for her being a young teenager who was still a virgin? It would be overwhelming!

HIS DIVINE PURPOSE—OUR SALVATION

The fact is, God sent Jesus from Heaven (John 8:16 and 8:18) to take on a physical body and go through all the temptations that we ourselves face, yet remaining sinless, and thereby sacrificing Himself for our transgressions so we may obtain grace (undeserved favor) in our weakness. Let us read the words in Hebrews 4:13-16:

> *And there is no creature hidden from His sight, but all things are open and laid bare to the eyes of Him with whom we have to do. Since then we have a great high priest who has passed through the heavens, Jesus the Son of God, let us hold fast our confession. For we do not have a high priest who cannot sympathize with our weakness, but One who has been tempted in all things as we are, yet without sin. Let us therefore draw near with confidence to the throne of grace, that we may receive mercy and may find grace to help in time of need.*

Not everyone will accept the sacrifice that Jesus made for us. Let us read the words written in the book of 1 Corinthians (1:18-21):

> *For the word of the cross is foolishness to those who are perishing, but to us who are being saved it is the power of God. For it is written, "I WILL DESTROY THE WISDOM OF THE WISE, AND THE CLEVERNESS OF THE CLEVER I WILL SET ASIDE." Where is the wise man? Where is the scribe? Where is the debater of this age? Has not God made foolish the wisdom of the world? For since in the wisdom of God the world through its wisdom did not come to know God, God was well-pleased through the foolishness of the message preached to save those who believe.*

And it continues in verse 25, *"Because the foolishness of God is wiser than men, and the weakness of God is stronger than men."*

And in 1 Corinthians 2:14-16 we read that we have the mind of Christ:

But a natural man does not accept the things of the Spirit of God; for they are foolishness to him, and he cannot understand them, because they are spiritually appraised. But he who is spiritual appraises all things, yet he himself is appraised by no one. For who "has known the mind of the Lord, that he will instruct Him?" But we have the mind of Christ.

Paul writes in 1 Corinthians, Chapter 3 verse 18-19 that the wisdom of the world is foolishness before God:

Let no man deceive himself. If any man among you thinks that he is wise in this age, he must first become foolish, so that he may become wise. For the wisdom of this world is foolishness before God.

Having heard these Scriptures, has your heart stirred within you? Can you hear the once distant inner voice whisper that all these words speak truth? Are you thirsty to learn more? If the answer is yes to any of these questions, then the Spirit of truth has revealed this to you and is already in your heart.

Jesus was not but a mere man, but was God incarnate and dwelt among us. That cannot be denied. It is written throughout all the Scriptures. God didn't have to send His Son more than once to defeat death, but He did send Him once…once for all. This is the good news; believe and receive His grace.

Let us go to the word of God for more answers. If we believe in Jesus, we are born of God. Whoever is born of God overcomes the world, in faith. The Spirit is truth. The Spirit bears witness of Jesus to us. When we believe in Jesus it's because we have the Spirit in our heart. The witness is that we have eternal life through the blood of Jesus. We can take this confidence before the throne of God knowing that whatever we ask, according to His will, is granted to us. Here are the recorded words found in the book of 1 John (5:1-15):

> *Whoever believes that Jesus is the Christ is born of God; and whoever loves the Father loves the child born of Him. By this we know that we love the children of God, when we love God and observe His commandments. For this is the love of God; that we keep His commandments; and His commandments are not burdensome. For whatever is born of God overcomes the world; and this is the victory that has overcome the world—our faith. And who is the one who overcomes the world, but he who believes that Jesus is the Son of God? This is the One who came by water and blood, Jesus Christ; not with the water only, but with the water and with the blood. And it is the Spirit who bears witness, because the Spirit is the truth. For there are three that bear witness; the Spirit and the water and the blood; and the three are in agreement. If we receive the witness of men, the witness of God is greater; for the witness of God is this, that He has borne witness concerning His Son. The one who believes in the Son of God has the witness in himself; the one who does not believe God has made Him a liar,*

because he has not believed in the witness that God has borne concerning His Son. And the witness is this, that God has given us eternal life, and this life is in His Son. He who has the Son has the life; he who does not have the Son of God does not have the life. These things I have written to you who believe in the name of the Son of God, in order that you may know that you have eternal life. And this is the confidence which we have before Him, that, if we ask anything according to His will, He hears us. And if we know that He hears us in whatever we ask, we know that we have the requests which we have asked from Him.

We are saved by grace through faith. This means that God's favor is on us even though we don't deserve it. God so loved us that He gave over His Son, Jesus, to men of sin that we might call upon His name and be saved. Jesus is the open door to the Father. Again, when we come before the Father with a repentant heart and He looks upon us, He no longer sees our sin, but instead sees His Son Jesus who paid the ultimate penalty with His life in exchange for our sins—that is true love, the gift of grace.

In Ephesians 2:1-10, we read about this as follows:

And you were dead in your trespasses and sins, in which you formerly walked according to the course of this world, according to the prince of the power of the air, of the spirit that is now working in the sons of disobedience. Among them we too all formerly lived in the lusts of our flesh, indulging the desires of the flesh and of the mind, and were by nature children of wrath, even as the rest. But God, being rich in mercy, because of His great love with which He loved us, even when we were dead in our transgressions, made us alive together with Christ (by grace you have been saved), and raised us up with Him, and seated us with Him in the heavenly places in Christ Jesus. For by grace you have been saved through faith; and that not of yourselves, it is the gift of God; not as a result of works, so that no one may boast. For we are His workmanship, created in Christ Jesus for good works, which God prepared beforehand, so that we would walk in them.

As we discussed earlier when Christ appeared, as the high priest, He entered the tabernacle and into the Holy of Holies to make a sacrifice on our behalf and to appear in the presence of God for us. Only He entered the true Holy of Holies in heaven, not the earthly representation, which was a mere copy. He did this not once a year, but "once for all" with His own blood sacrifice, that being much more precious than the blood of calves and goats. We read God's word in Hebrews 9:11-28:

But when Christ appeared as a high priest of the good things to come, He entered through the greater and more perfect tabernacle, not made with hands, that is to say, not of this creation; and not through the blood of goats and calves, but through His own blood, He entered the holy place "once for all," having obtained eternal redemption. For if the blood of goats and bulls and the ashes of a heifer sprinkling those who have been defiled, sanctify for the cleansing of the flesh, how much more will the blood of Christ, who through the eternal Spirit offered Himself without blemish to God, cleanse your conscience from dead works to serve the living God? And for this reason He is the mediator of a new covenant, in order that since a death has taken place for the redemption of the transgressions that were committed under the first covenant, those who have been called may receive the promise of the eternal inheritance. For where a covenant is, there must of necessity be the death of the one who made it. For a covenant is valid only when men are dead, for it is never in force while the one who made it lives. Therefore even the first covenant was not inaugurated without blood. For when every commandment had been spoken by Moses to all the people according to the Law, he took the blood of the calves and the goats, with water and scarlet wool and hyssop, and sprinkled both the book itself and all the people, saying, "THIS IS THE BLOOD OF THE COVENANT WHICH GOD COMMANDED YOU." And in the same way he sprinkled both the tabernacle and all the vessels of the ministry with the blood. And according to the Law, one may almost say, all things are cleansed with blood, and without shedding of blood there is no forgiveness. Therefore it was necessary for the copies of the things in the heavens to be cleansed with these, but the heavenly things themselves with better sacrifices than these. For Christ did not enter a holy place made with hands, a mere copy of the true one, but into heaven itself, now to appear in the presence of God for us; nor was it that He should offer Himself often, as the high priest enters the holy place year by year with blood not his own. Otherwise, He would have needed to suffer often since the foundation of the world; but now once at the consummation of the ages He has been manifested to put away sin by the sacrifice of Himself. And inasmuch as it is appointed for men to die once and after this comes judgment, so Christ also, having been offered once to bear the sins of the many, shall appear a second time for salvation without reference to sin, to those who eagerly await Him.

The verses above state that, *"…it is appointed for men to die once and after this comes judgment…"* Not twice or three times, but once, just as Christ died once. However, He will appear a second time, in His resurrected body, for our salvation, *"…without reference to sin, to those who eagerly await Him."*

In the book of John (5:24) we read that when we believe in Him, we are not judged. After hearing these words, there is no way that I would risk facing an eternity in the absence of His love and salvation:

Truly, truly, I say to you, he who hears My word, and believes Him who sent Me, has eternal life, and does not come into judgment, but has passed out of death into life.

I think by now no one can deny that we have eternal life in Jesus. By simply hearing the word of Jesus and believing God the Father who sent Him, we have eternal life. That is cause for celebration, because He made it readily available to all who believe.

My Personal Testimony

Jesus is the Word, the Creator, the only begotten Son of God, the Light of the world; He is God, in the flesh…God the Son, Jesus. Anyone who denies this truth, is not of God, but of the world. If you're not sure, that's okay, but you should ask to be enlightened to the truth. Ask for the truth to be made known to you, and you will receive. However, don't be disappointed if you don't receive the answer right away. For me it took two years for Him to reveal Himself to me after asking to know the truth about Him. You might get the answer right away, I'm only saying don't be disappointed if it takes longer.

I'm here to testify that, in fact, Jesus was not just a mere man, but was God incarnate and now is sitting at the right hand of God the Father. He has sent His Holy Spirit to comfort and teach us. Jesus is our intercessor to the Father. As the Father looks upon those who have accepted the sacrifice Jesus made for them, He only sees His Son Jesus. Therefore, there is no condemnation for all the awful things that we did. There is absolutely no doubt in me to this truth, and I'm willing to die rather than to deny His name.

In my early twenties, coming out of the military during the Vietnam era and like so many others, I tried to find myself. In forming my own belief system, I found conflict with the spiritual teachings of my youth. My flesh was warring with my inner spirit, like the worldly views fighting with my good conscience.

You see, my father and mother planted a seed in me when I was very young. It was the seed of truth. Seldom did I water it, if ever. I was in the world and experiencing the things of the world for the first time, so it didn't interest me. In time, the conflict within me, between truth and the world grew. Deep inside, the seed whispered truths to me, but the voice of the world was much louder and more exciting. To my benefit, the seed planted those many years before by my loving parents, never completely died out for lack of water.

Often I found myself balanced on the edge of right and wrong sometimes slipping off to the left and sometimes to the right, but I always scraped my way back to the edge trying to maintain the balance.

While yet in the military, I had a dream that caused a great conflict within my mind. As I faced a dark stairwell, an immense dog great dane to be exact, loped toward me. My first thought was to flee for my life, but it was even darker behind me than facing the large animal, so I offered my right hand and slightly bent over. He brushed by my hand, turned and went over to a table, sat down and looked up at his master. It was then I realized the dogs master was a demon. Instantly, I was filled with terror! Without hesitating, I screamed the name of "Jesus!" From the center of my vision, an intensely bright light instantly engulfed me, and I awoke.

This of course puzzled me, because I had told myself that I didn't believe, yet in the moment I feared for my life I called out His name, and He came to my rescue. I was in a state of turmoil from that moment on.

In 1972, soon after I was discharged from the military, I spent much of my time walking the streets of Boulder, Colorado, up on the "Hill". This was on the west side of the University of Colorado Boulder campus and was a very cool place where there were lots of girls, head shops, loud rock music, hippies, and of course, drugs were prevalent. It was the "in crowd" and I wanted to be a part of it. Oddly enough, in that environment a long haired hippie approached me on the sidewalk preaching Jesus Christ to me.

To hear the name of Jesus was like nails on a chalk board, and I wanted him to leave me alone. So I said something to shut him up, and when he wouldn't, I scurried away hoping no one would notice. The words he spoke were like daggers in my heart. It was as if his words reached the seed my parents planted with life-giving water. It sprouted forth pushing against my chest causing conflict with the worldly mind I'd adopted.

After that experience, I tried to forget it ever happened. But the burning turmoil in my mind and the desire to know the truth continued to haunt me, until one day I couldn't stand it anymore—I had to know the truth. I shouted out this question, "Jesus, if you are real, reveal yourself to me and only then will I believe and follow after you."

Two years later on a frigid late winter night early in 1974, something incredible happened to me. My brother Joe, having been a part of the Charismatic movement within the Catholic Church, invited me to view a movie he was showing in his home later that evening. Now I knew the crowd he hung with, and I really didn't want any part of that pious group. So I made a deal with him. I would only come if I could come exactly at the hour the movie started and could leave the minute it was over without having to speak with anyone. He agreed.

The movie was "Like a Thief in the Night," by Mark IV Pictures. I was engrossed in it. It touched my soul and as promised, my brother helped me scoot out afterwards without having to speak with anyone.

When I got out to the car, the windshield was completely iced over, so I started the engine and decided to sit there while the defroster slowly melted the ice off in order to contemplate the movie I had just seen. I wanted no distraction as I tried to discern what was happening to me. My life flashed in front of me as I reflected back on the sin that had so entangled my life. I felt a sense of deep remorse for all the evil things I had done throughout my life and felt the heaviness of shame. I wanted to be cleansed of it all.

In that moment, I envisioned my 'being' as a house. Depending on how much I trusted someone would depend on how far I would take them into my house. As in the case of Jesus, I had in the past, invited Him into the living room and would allow Him to go no farther for fear He would see something that would embarrass me. But this time it was different; this time I gave Him free access to everything including the closets where I kept many of the secrets I had hidden in shame. This time, however, I gladly gave Him free access and asked Him, begged Him, to clean it out, top to bottom.

As I waited for the windshield to clear, I sat there sobbing with deep heart wrenching sobs from the inner most part of my being. As the tears gushed from my eyes, so did the pain, conflict, and turmoil that had so entangled me. With each sob, my soul became lighter and less troubled. Although it was cold outside, I was overcome with warmth that comforted and permeated my heart while my house was being cleansed. I felt wrapped in a blanket of love, like I have never before felt. My life was a wreck, but now I had confessed to the Son of God all of my deepest and darkest secrets, and he replaced them with His love and a total sense of forgiveness. As I pulled away from the curb and headed for home, the tears still running down my face, I reflected back on what had just taken place with a thankful attitude; I was free and at peace for the first time in my life.

The next morning, I awoke a new man, transformed from the inside out. I realized I had not only met Jesus, but the prayer I had prayed two years earlier was answered. His Spirit was in me filling my heart with His love. The newness was overwhelming. I found a peace in myself that cannot be totally described. I found myself happy to be alive and a love for people…all people…no matter what they looked like, no matter how they were dressed and no matter the circumstances, I loved all people. I wanted eagerly to tell everyone of my new found peace, like the hippie on the hill in Boulder, Colorado had done to me some years earlier.

What I found was the same rejection I had given the hippie on the hill, but do you know what, it didn't matter. I had a peace that passes all worldly understanding and nothing could take that from me. For six months, I was filled with this new found peace and love. I had the Light of the world filling me completely and it shined forth from my being like living waters.

To achieve perfection, on our own is literally impossible. We may strive for perfection and we may get very close, but there will always be a flaw, or we will always miss the perfect mark in some way. This is why people develop contingency plans because of the unknown factors that affect the results of our striving for perfection. I might add, this applies to our relationships as well.

We constantly deal with our pride, self centeredness, our wants and desires, past experiences, and our imperfections. We have an enemy who knows how we will react to any given situation in order to keep us from achieving a perfect and harmonious relationship with our Savior.

There is only one person, however, who reached perfection and whom was the manifestation of perfection Himself; having never made a mistake, or said the wrong thing, nor stumbled in His walk to achieve His divine mission. He faced the same challenges and temptations of life as we do to the point of shedding His blood. But He was in direct harmony with His Father's will. He didn't rely on the flesh, but looked toward the Father for all things and conquered the flesh. He set the standard for us that we may learn from Him and the words He spoke in order to receive His grace, His love, and His perfection in our hearts that we may show others in order that they may see and be saved as well.

We are only human and subject to imperfection. However, if we lift up our prayers to the Father, having these imperfections we may stumble and fall occasionally until we learn to rely on Him for all things. The perfection we seek is only attainable through His son Jesus, the Morning Star (Revelation 22:16).

Remember, in Jeremiah 1:5 we are told that He knew us before He formed us in the womb, *"Before I formed you in the womb I knew you, and before you were born I consecrated you…"* He knows everything about you.

Let me remind you again the words recorded in Ephesians 1:4, which makes it clear that we existed before coming to this earth, even if you were just a thought in the mind of our Lord, *"just as He chose us in Him before the foundation of the world."* There is no coincidence that you are reading this book right now—He chose you in Him.

Let us be encouraged by the words that Jesus spoke to His disciples, after His death and resurrection, but before His ascension into heaven, and were recorded in the book of Mathew (28:18):

Chapter 3

And Jesus came up and spoke to them, saying, "All authority has been given to Me in heaven and on earth. Go therefore and make disciples of all the nations, baptizing them in the name of the Father, and the Son and the Holy Spirit, teaching them to observe all that I commanded you; and lo, I am with you always, even to the end of the age.

Chapter 4

THE HOLY SPIRIT: THE COMFORTER

The first time we hear of the Holy Spirit in the Scriptures is in the second verse of Genesis 1:2, *"…and the Spirit of God was moving over the surface of the waters…"* which was during the creation of the world. The word used for the Creator here is *"Elohim,"* which, in the Hebrew is the plural use of the Godhead; plural yet one, where *"El"* means the strong God.

Although in the Old Testament there isn't much said about the Trinity, in the New Testament it is much more clearly stated. Still, it remains a mystery and requires faith to believe in our Triune God; the Father, the Son, and the Holy Spirit.

As I was writing this chapter, the Holy Spirit brought these words to my heart:

Chapter 4

> IN OUR HEART
> Holy Father, Holy Son
> Holy Spirit, three as One
> By Your word we see it so
> With eyes open we will know
> It is by faith we believe
> In our heart, You so weave _{JAG 10/08}

It might help to think of our own makeup having a body (Hebrew word, "Basar" which means: flesh), a soul or being (Hebrew word, "Nephesh" which means: living being, life, self, person, desire, passion, appetite, emotions), and a spirit (Hebrew word, "Ruach" which means: breath, wind, spirit).

Now we also have an inner man spoken of in the Old Testament and referred to as heart (Hebrew word, "Leb" or "Lebab" which means: inner man, mind, will, heart). We are one, yet having all these distinct parts.

Who is the Spirit of God? He is the third person in the trinity. He is the power of God. He is truth. He is the Helper. He is the Comforter. He is Teacher. He is the one who sanctifies us. He is the breath of God—the Spirit of God. Without Him we will not understand the Scriptures. Without Him we will not come to know God the Father or God the Son. He is an integral part of our triune God. He intercedes for the Father and the Son and comes into our heart.

It is for Our Benefit

Let's read the words of Jesus when speaking of the Holy Spirit, the Helper, recorded in the book of John 14:25-26:

> *These things I have spoken to you while abiding with you. But the Helper, the Holy Spirit, whom the Father will send in My name, He will teach you all things, and bring to your remembrance all that I said to you.*

In John 15:26-27, we read the words that Jesus spoke to His disciples, *"When the Helper comes whom I will send to you from the Father, that is the Spirit of truth who proceeds from the Father, He will testify about Me…"* Here we see that Jesus will send the Spirit of truth who proceeds from the Father. We also see this in John 14:16-17.

We know that it is to our advantage that Jesus died for our sins on the cross and was resurrected in life. For had He not, He would not have sent the Holy Spirit to us. We see this in the words Jesus continued speaking to His disciples in the book of John (16:5-15):

> *But now I am going to Him who sent Me; and none of you asks Me, "Where are you going?" But because I have said these things to you, sorrow has filled your heart. But I tell you the truth, it is to your advantage that I go away; for if I do not go away, the Helper will not come to you; but if I go, I will send Him to you. And He, when He comes, will convict the world concerning righteousness, because I go to the Father and you no longer see Me; and concerning judgment, because the ruler of this world has been judged. I have many more things to say to you, but*

> *you cannot bear them now. But when He, the Spirit of truth, comes, He will guide you into all the truth; for He will not speak on His own initiative, but whatever He hears, He will speak; and He will disclose to you what is to come. He will glorify Me, for He will take of Mine and will disclose it to you. All things that the Father has are mine; therefore I said that He takes of Mine and will disclose it to you.*

Immaculate Conception by the Holy Spirit

We read in a previous chapter about the virgin birth of our Lord. But did you realize it was by the Holy Spirit that Mary became pregnant with Jesus. We see evidence of this in the book of Mathew (1:18-20):

> *Now the birth of Jesus Christ was as follows. When His mother Mary had been betrothed to Joseph, before they came together she was found to be with child by the Holy Spirit. And Joseph her husband, being a righteous man, and not wanting to disgrace her, desired to put her away secretly. But when he had considered this, behold, an angel of the Lord appeared to him in a dream, saying, "Joseph, son of David, do not be afraid to take Mary as your wife; for that which has been conceived in her is of the Holy Spirit.*

It may be difficult for you to understand how this could be possible, but that is because we think in human terms, which limits the possibilities. But God is supernatural and is not restricted by carnal thinking. Once we accept this fact, it will make it easier for us to believe. Incredibly, we will be more open to receive increased knowledge, faith and more importantly, the blessings God intends for us. It's our carnal thinking that keeps us from believing miracles are possible. Let us not forget, with God all things are possible (Mathew19:26) to those that believe.

Unpardonable Sin

We read that although our sins are forgiven through Jesus, there is one sin that will not be forgiven; it is unpardonable. Let's turn to the book of John (12:31-32) where Jesus speaks of this:

> *Therefore I say to you, any sin and blasphemy shall be forgiven men, but blasphemy against the Spirit shall not be forgiven. And whoever shall speak a word against the Son of Man, it shall be forgiven him; but whoever shall speak against the Holy Spirit, it shall not be forgiven him, either in this age, or in the age to come.*

Let us take these words seriously because God chooses His words well. We can speak words against Him or His Son, but not against His Spirit. "Thank you Father, for your words of warning," should be our response to Him in respect. It would be well for us to pay heed to His words.

The Infilling of the Holy Spirit

All through both the Old Testament and the New Testament

Scriptures we read of the presence of the Holy Spirit. An example of this can be found as we read Psalms 51:11. David was dependant and comforted by the Holy Spirit and asked God not to take the Spirit from him, *"Do not cast me away from Thy presence, and do not take Thy Holy Spirit from me."*

In Isaiah 63:8-14, 17, we read the account of how God favored the house of Israel, but they rebelled against Him and grieved His Holy Spirit. He therefore turned away from them, but they suddenly realized this remembering how He had been with them in the days of Moses. Then they returned to Him once again:

> *For He said, "surely, they are My people, Sons who will not deal falsely." So He became their Savior. In all their affliction He was afflicted, and the angel of His presence saved them; In His love and in His mercy He redeemed them; and He lifted them and carried them all the days of old.*
>
> *But they rebelled and grieved His Holy Spirit; therefore, He turned Himself to become their enemy, He fought against them. Then His people remembered the days of old, of Moses. Where is He who brought them up out of the sea with the shepherds of His flock? Where is He who put His Holy Spirit in the midst of them? Who caused His glorious arm to go at the right hand of Moses, who divided the waters before them to make for Himself an everlasting name, who led them through the depths? Like the horse in the wilderness, they did not stumble; as*

> *the cattle which go down into the valley, the Spirit of the Lord gave them rest…*
>
> *v.17, Why, O Lord, dost Thou cause us to stray from Thy ways, and harden our heart from fearing Thee? Return for the sake of Thy servants, the tribes of Thy heritage.*

We read in Luke 1:15 that John the Baptist was filled with the Holy Spirit while yet in his mothers womb, *"For he will be great in the sight of the Lord, and he will drink no wine or liquor; and he will be filled with the Holy Spirit, while yet in his mother's womb."*

Elizabeth, the mother of John the Baptist, was filled with the Holy Spirit when she heard the greeting of Mary, the mother of Jesus, on a visit. Even before Mary uttered a word, Elizabeth also recognized that she had become pregnant with the Son of God. This could only have happened by revelation from the Holy Spirit. Let's read the account given in Luke 1:36-43 that starts with the words of the angel that visited Mary announcing her pregnancy by the Holy Spirit:

> *"And behold, even your relative Elizabeth has also conceived a son in her old age; and she who was called barren is now in her sixth month. For nothing will be impossible with God." And Mary said, "behold, the bondslave of the Lord; be it done to me according to your word." And the angel departed from her. Now at this time Mary arose and went with haste to the hill country, to a city of Judah, and entered the house of Zacharias*

and greeted Elizabeth. And it came about that when Elizabeth heard Mary's greeting, the baby leaped in her womb; and Elizabeth was filled with the Holy Spirit. And she cried out with a loud voice, and said, "Blessed among women are you, and blessed is the fruit of your womb! And how has it happened to me, that the mother of my Lord should come to me? For behold, when the sound of your greeting reached my ears, the baby leaped in my womb for joy...."

Jesus was also filled with the Holy Spirit as He was baptized by John the Baptist. We read the account in Luke 3:21-22:

Now it came about when all the people were baptized, that Jesus also was baptized, and while He was praying, heaven was opened, and the Holy Spirit descended upon Him in bodily form like a dove, and a voice came out of heaven, "Thou are My beloved Son, in Thee I am well-pleased."

After Jesus had been crucified and was resurrected, He appeared to His disciples and commanded them to go out and make disciples of all the nations, baptizing them in the name of the Father and the Son and the Holy Spirit. His words were recorded in the book of Mathew (28:16-20):

But the eleven disciples proceeded to Galilee, to the mountain which Jesus had designated. And when they saw Him, they worshiped Him; but some were

> *doubtful. And Jesus came up and spoke to them, saying, "All authority has been given to Me in heaven and on earth. Go therefore and make disciples of all the nations, baptizing them in the name of the Father and the Son and the Holy Spirit, teaching them to observe all that I commanded you; and lo, I am with you always, even to the end of the age."*

God intended from the beginning that we have the Holy Spirit. The Holy Spirit has always been made available to those that turn to Him and aspire to walk with Him daily. If we don't have the Holy Spirit in our hearts, it is because of our choice alone. For it requires total submission to the Lord in order to receive the Holy Spirit. Being lukewarm will never do! You must in all sincerity will it with your whole being. You must be on fire for Him!

Do not depend on your feelings, for feelings can deceive. If you've invited Jesus into your heart, know that His Spirit is there whether you feel it or not. I have found that as I turn my awareness toward Him throughout the day, His Spirit is manifested to my knowledge. He had been there all along, but in the hustle and bustle of life I wasn't paying attention.

Also know that the enemy wants to keep you from walking daily with the Spirit. The enemy does not want you to have the joy of the Lord in your heart. Remember though that the enemy has been defeated at the cross and he has no hold on you anymore; unless you give him one. Praise God!!!

The Spirit Will Guide Your Words

In the book of Mark (13:11), Jesus is speaking to His disciples and comforting them saying, when you are arrested, do not be anxious in what you will say, because the Holy Spirit will speak for you:

And when they arrest you and deliver you up, do not be anxious beforehand about what you are to say, but say whatever is given you in that hour; for it is not you who speak, but it is the Holy Spirit.

We can take this into almost any crisis situation we may be facing and lift up our needs in prayer to the Father that His Holy Spirit would guide our words and He will honor our prayer. The Holy Spirit will give us the words in that hour of crisis, no matter how small, just as he did for Christians throughout biblical history.

In chapter one, we discussed the Scriptures being written by men, but inspired by God. In support of this truth, Scriptures were referenced. However, not all the Scriptures were listed. In Acts 1:16 we read that the Holy Spirit foretold through the mouth of David, a prophet of God:

Brethren, the Scripture had to be fulfilled, which the Holy Spirit foretold by the mouth of David concerning Judas, who became a guide to those who arrested Jesus.

And again in Mark 12:37, Jesus answered the questions of the scribes and quoted Old Testament Scripture, which He did on many occasions. In this case, He clarified His deity through the words given by the Holy Spirit to David as follows:

> *And Jesus answering began to say, as He taught in the temple, "How is it that the scribes say that the Christ is the son of David? David himself said in the Holy Spirit, 'THE LORD SAID TO MY LORD, SIT AT MY RIGHT HAND, UNTIL I PUT THINE ENEMIES BENEATH THY FEET.' David himself calls Him 'LORD;' and so in what sense is He his son?"*

Furthermore, in the book of 2 Timothy (1:19-21) we read:

> *And so we have the prophetic word made more sure, to which you do well to pay attention as to a lamp shining in a dark place, until the day dawns and the morning star arises in your hearts. But know this first of all, that no prophecy of Scripture is a matter of one's own interpretation, for no prophesy was ever made by an act of human will, but men moved by the Holy Spirit spoke from God.*

No prophesy is made by an act of human will, but is by men moved by the Holy Spirit spoke from God. This applies with those who read the Scriptures as well. It is by the Holy Spirit that we come to understand them. It's a wonderful thing to be directed, guided and moved by the Holy Spirit. We will hear His ever present soft voice if we would only listen.

The Spirit of God is a Gift

We are told that we shall receive the Holy Spirit when we repent and are baptized in the name of Jesus Christ for the forgiveness of our sins. It doesn't say that we may receive the Holy Spirit, but instead it states that we shall receive the gift of the Holy Spirit. In Acts 2:38 we read the God inspired words of Peter:

> *And Peter said to them, "Repent, and let each of you be baptized in the name of Jesus Christ for the forgiveness of your sins; and you shall receive the gift of the Holy Spirit."*

We read in the book of Acts (19:1-7), that disciples in Ephesus who had been baptized in the name of John, had not received the gift of the Holy Spirit. When Paul heard this, He baptized them in the name of Jesus laying hands on them, and they instantly received the Holy Spirit:

> *And it came about that while Apollos was at Corinth, Paul having passed through the upper country came to Ephesus, and found some disciples, and he said to them, "Did you receive the Holy Spirit when you believed?" And they said to him, "No, we have not even heard whether there is a Holy Spirit." And he said , "Into what then were you baptized?" And they said, "Into John's baptism." And Paul said, "John baptized with the baptism of repentance, telling the people to believe in Him who was coming after him, that is, in Jesus." And*

when they heard this, they were baptized in the name of the Lord Jesus. And when Paul had laid his hands upon them, the Holy Spirit came on them, and they began speaking with tongues and prophesying. And there were in all about twelve men.

The Love of God has been poured out within our hearts through the Holy Spirit. In the book of Romans (5:1-5) we are given this knowledge:

Therefore, having been justified by faith, we have peace with God through our Lord Jesus Christ, through whom also we have obtained our introduction by faith into this grace in which we stand; and we exult in hope of the glory of God. And not only this, but we also exult in our tribulations, knowing that tribulation brings about perseverance; and perseverance, proven character,; and proven character, hope; and hope does not disappoint, because the love of God has been poured out within our hearts through the Holy Spirit who was given to us.

Again, I emphasize the Hebrew word "Ruach" meaning, "breath, wind and spirit." Throughout the Old Testament theologians used this word for Spirit countless times. This same Hebrew word is also used in reference to the Spirit of God, the Spirit of Life, the Spirit of the Lord, and the Spirit of wisdom. However, it is only capitalized when used in reference to God or His Spirit.

However, we also see the same Hebrew word "Ruach"

(spirit) interchanged for the word "breath" as used in the "breath of life" (Genesis 6:7, 7:15) when referring to both men and animals. This doesn't mean that animals are on the same level as people, because there is Scripture that clearly places man above all creation on the earth (Genesis 1:28), but then we shouldn't be surprised either.

Often times in the Old Testament we read, *"the Spirit of God came upon him,"* or *"the Spirit of the Lord came mightily upon him,"* or *"was upon him,"* which allowed simple men to do great things. One such example of this can be found in Judges 3:10:

> *And the Spirit of the Lord came upon him, and he judged Israel. When he went out to war, the Lord gave Cushan-rishathaim king of Mesopotamia into his hand, so that he prevailed over Cushan-rishathaim.*

In Judges, chapter 6, 7 and 8, it is recorded that the Spirit of the Lord came over Gideon in order to deliver the enemies of Israel into his hand, but wanted all to know that it was God behind the victory so the people would not boast thinking it was their might and with their power. This account leaves no doubt that the Lord's Spirit was making it possible.

The full account of this story starts with chapter six, but I will start with verse 33 in the sixth book of Judges where the Spirit of God came over Gideon, *"So the Spirit of the Lord came upon Gideon; and he blew a trumpet, and the Abiezrites were called together to follow him."* Then we jump to Judges 7:2-4:

And the Lord said to Gideon, "The people who are with you are too many for Me to give Midian into their hands, lest Israel become boastful, saying, 'My own power has delivered me.' Now therefore come, proclaim in the hearing of the people, saying, whoever, is afraid and trembling, let him return and depart from Mount Gilead." So 22,000 people returned, but 10,000 remained. Then the Lord said to Gideon, "The people are still too many; bring them down to the water and I will test them for you there. Therefore, it shall be that he of whom I say to you, 'This one shall go with you, he shall go with you; but everyone of whom I say to you, 'This one shall not go with you,' he shall not go."

After this was done, there only remained 300 men. And the Lord chose those men out of the remaining 10,000 warriors. Then the Lord told Gideon to take his servant and go down to the enemy's camp and spy out what they are saying. So Gideon did as he was instructed by the Lord.

It is recorded that at the enemy's camp written in Judges 7:12, *"Now the Midianites and the Amalekites and all the sons of the east were lying in the valley as numerous as locusts; and their camels were without number, as numerous as the sand on the seashore."*

Gideon learned what the Lord wanted him to hear, as one of the Midian soldiers spoke of a dream he had and another soldier interpreted the dream for his friend. The dream confirmed that Gideon and Israel would prevail over them in war. So Gideon returned to his own camp and worshiped the Lord and professed victory over the Midians.

Gideon separated the 300 men into three groups with each man bearing a trumpet. During the night they went down to the valley where all 300 men blew their trumpets. The Midian army being confused ran in all directions and started fighting each other. They fled before the 300 in a state of fear. Gideon later prevailed over them, as it had been foretold and he gave all the glory to God.

There are so many supernatural accounts like Gideon's, there isn't paper to write it all down. But suffice to say, when the Spirit of the Lord comes upon you, you will be able to do extraordinary supernatural things which would otherwise be impossible by our human limitations.

The Temple of the Holy Spirit

We are told that when you are married to another you become one flesh with your partner. We see this is so in Mark 10:6-8 (referencing Genesis 1:27, 5:2) where Jesus is speaking to the crowds:

> *But from the beginning of creation, God,* "MADE THEM MALE AND FEMALE. FOR THIS CAUSE A MAN SHALL LEAVE HIS FATHER AND MOTHER, AND THE TWO SHALL BECOME ONE FLESH." *consequently, they are no longer two, but one flesh.*

Even if you aren't married, and you are joined with another, you still become one. We see this to be true in the book of 1

Corinthians 6:16, *"Or do you not know that the one who joins himself to a harlot is one body with her? For He says, 'THE TWO WILL BECOME ONE FLESH.'"*

Why then are you surprised that when you are joined to another there is so much emotion tied to it? Did you not know your body is the temple of the Holy Spirit? Let's read the words of the Holy Spirit through Paul in 1 Corinthians 6:17-20 where it is explained in more detail:

> *But the one who joins himself to the Lord is one spirit with Him. Flee immorality. Every other sin that a man commits is outside the body, but the immoral man sins against his own body. Or do you not know that your body is a temple of the Holy Spirit who is in you, whom you have from God, and that you are not your own? For you have been bought with a price; therefore glorify God in your body.*

Reliance on the Holy Spirit; Where All Talents Come From

In the book of Exodus, chapter 31, the Lord spoke to Moses and explained that He was responsible, through His Spirit, for giving wisdom, knowledge, understanding, and He gave talents to certain men having specific tasks to perform according to His will, to those willing. He specifically states that this occurs, *"with the Spirit of God."* So let's take a look at how it is stated in Exodus 31:1-5:

> *Now the Lord spoke to Moses, saying, "See, I have called by name Bezalel, the son of Uri, the son of Hur, of the*

> *tribe of Judah. And I have filled him with the Spirit of God in wisdom, in understanding, in knowledge, and in all kinds of craftsmanship, to make artistic designs for work in gold, in silver, and in bronze, and in cutting of stones for settings, and in the carving of wood, that he may work in all kinds of craftsmanship."*

The thing is, each of us can ask for the help of the Holy Spirit and it will be granted to us. In Luke 11:13, the words of Jesus were recorded:

> *If you then, being evil, know how to give good gifts to your children, how much more shall your heavenly Father give the Holy Spirit to those who ask Him?*

When you willingly open your heart to the Holy Spirit through Jesus, you will be transformed. Christ will be in your heart, the temple of God will be in your heart, and His power will work through you from the inside out by His Holy Spirit. People may not understand what it is they see, but they will like what they see. God's favor will be on you. You will be an example and others will want what you have to His glory. Here are the words of Jesus that were recorded in Mathew 5:13, 14, 16:

> (v. 13)...*You are the salt of the earth...*
> (v. 14)...*You are the light of the world...*
> (v. 16)...*Let your light shine before men in such a way that they may see your good works, and glorify your Father who is in heaven.*

For this to happen, we must die to the flesh, not literally, but figuratively. The flesh is anything that draws us away from the Spirit, including anything that is related to self. So we must learn to curb self and not lust after money, for instance, or sex or food to the point that we over indulge or think too highly of ourselves. We must be more humble and less prideful. We must temper everything that causes us to lose self control and turn instead to the Spirit for all things. We must learn to rely on the Spirit for everything. It is a learned dependency. This is not easy if you're anything like me, whereby you have learned to depend on yourself and you don't ask anyone for help.

This is why I say 'It is a learned dependency,' because it may take a lifetime to learn. I find myself worrying about this and that, and trying to solve this or that without ever thinking of going to God for help and placing my trust in Him to solve the little problems. You see, if you just turn the problem over to Him, the Spirit will work out the details, and you will have your answer on how to solve the problem in less time with no worry. This I know to be true, but getting myself accustomed to handing all the problems over to the Lord is yet another thing.

We are told not to depend on our own understanding. And as we learn to trust in Him, He promises to make our paths straight, as we see in the book of Proverbs (3:5-6):

> *Trust in the Lord with all your heart, and do not lean on your own understanding. In all your ways acknowledge Him, and He will make your paths straight.*

The word "acknowledge" in the verse above is the Hebrew word "yada" and is used in a great variety of senses. It means more than our word acknowledge may indicate. It actually means to know by observing and reflecting on, to know by experiencing, to perceive; as with a familiar friend or kinsfolk, for a certainty to understand and comprehend and to have knowledge of and also to have respect for. I could go on and on, but I think you get the point. It is a word that has much more meaning than just to acknowledge someone as you may enter a room. We should attentively seek Him out in all things, and He will make our paths straight.

What does that mean, to make our paths straight? It means He will go before us and work out all the details to make what we are doing doable. In another words, He will make everything work out to our benefit for His glory.

What an incredible revelation. How wonderful it is when the Spirit opens the eyes of our heart to know the truth of the Scriptures and the passing of wisdom to us as we study His Word. In Proverbs 3:13-26 we read:

> *How blessed is the man who finds wisdom, and the man who gains knowledge. For its profit is better than the profit of silver, and its gain than fine gold. She is more precious than jewels; and nothing you desire compares with her. Long life is in her right hand; in her left hand are riches and honor. Her ways are pleasant ways, and all her paths are peace. She is a tree of life to those who take hold of her, and happy are all who hold her fast. The*

Lord by wisdom founded the earth; by understanding He established the heavens. By His knowledge the deeps were broken up, and the skies drip with dew. My son, let them not depart from your sight; keep sound wisdom and discretion, so they will be life to your soul, and adornment to your neck. Then you will walk in your way securely, and your foot will not stumble. When you lie down, you will not be afraid; when you lie down, your sleep will be sweet. Do not be afraid of sudden fear, nor of the onslaught of the wicked when it comes; for the Lord will be your confidence, and will keep your foot from being caught.

Don't reject the gift of His Holy Spirit, because it will be a rejection of God Himself. Instead open your heart to His mercy, repent with a sincere heart and accept the sacrifice Jesus made for you. You will receive His gift of grace and the gift of the Holy Spirit which will fill your heart with His joy, like you've never experienced before.

COME LORD FILL MY HEART
Jesus, forgive me my weaknesses,
Remove my doubts and all my fears,
Help me to trust in you for all things,
Protect me from the enemy,
And send Your Spirit to fill my heart,
With Your perfect Love. JAG 2009

Chapter 5

FAITH OF A MUSTARD SEED

Do you believe that the sun will come up every morning, rain or shine? Do you believe that the gravity of the earth will keep you pinned to the ground day in and day out? The fact is we all have faith that these things will take place to the point that we don't even think about them. We take these things for granted.

Everyone has faith about something. Even the one who believes in the theory of evolution is accepting that in faith. You may be saying right now that this isn't faith because faith has to do with religion. And I would agree the common use for the word, faith, has been primarily religious in nature. But to truly understand how much of what we believe in is done in faith, we need only look at the definition.

The Oxford dictionary defines faith as, "complete trust or confidence," while Webster's definition is, "confident belief in the truth, value, or trustworthiness of a person, idea, or thing." Neither of these definitions have anything to do with religion. Are you beginning to see how faith is very much a part of our belief system?

Let's read how God's Word defines faith in the book of Hebrews (11:1), *"Faith is the assurance of things hoped for, the conviction of things not seen."* Contemplate those words for a moment, because there is understanding and wisdom in them.

Faith and the Word

Where does faith come from? In Romans 10:17, it states *"So faith comes from hearing, and hearing by the Word of Christ."* This is why it's so important to read the Word. If you want more faith, read the Word of God, and it will be given unto you by the Holy Spirit through Christ.

We are also told that we should live by faith, for by faith men of old gained God's approval. As Paul writes in Hebrews 11:2-3:

> *For by it the men of old gained approval. By faith we understand that the worlds were prepared by the Word of God, so that what is seen was not made out of things which are visible.*

Determination, Positive Thinking and Setting Our Minds on the Spirit

Being the second born in my family, I tried harder to achieve success than my older brother because I had to in order to prove my worth. My brother was three and a half years older than me and got to do so much more than I was allowed to do. My father would let him drive the tractor, for example, but I was too small. I didn't see the difference, but my father did. That had a profound affect on me. I grew up thinking I was something less than what I believed I was. However, I was not going to settle for second best. It made me strive harder to prove my worth; I had to prove I could measure up. I tried harder, and therefore got a determined attitude about everything I did. In this way, my father would recognize my abilities and let me drive the tractor, so to speak.

I excelled in everything that I set my mind at achieving. I was in little league playing baseball, for example. By the third year I was hitting home runs. No one could climb a tree faster than me…no one. In grade school in our gym class, I was one of the fastest runners. I say 'one of the fastest,' because in truth, I was the second fastest. My friend, Jerrold was the fastest. No matter how many times I raced him, I couldn't beat him. I was always a step behind him because he could get off the line quicker than me. I may not have always been the best, but I was sure trying to be.

Later in high school, I continued to have success. I was determined to master the trampoline and was the best in our class and school being able to do triple front flips. I found these much more difficult than triple back flips. I set a school record for extended push ups at 134 (fully extended arms out past my head while laying flat on my stomach and push up with my hands and toes). Only one person could climb a rope faster than me, my friend Jim Stewart. I was only a split second slower, but just as in the case with Jerrold a few years earlier no matter how hard I tried I couldn't beat him. The point I'm trying to make is that I learned to have faith in myself with each realized achievement or even as in some of the cases a near victory; it was all about faith.

Yes, faith can be learned through determined attitude and successful experience. With each victory we tend to believe in ourselves a little bit more. We may find that we are second best, at times, but it doesn't stop us from striving for that number one slot.

Having faith is like having a positive attitude. No one hit a home run by thinking negatively. You may have been surprised when you actually hit a home run, but at the very least, you had hope. If you thought negatively, believe me you would not have been able to clear the fence. Having a positive mind set is the difference between having success and experiencing failure.

You may have faith in your own abilities. In fact, if you believe with a strong enough conviction, you will actually succeed in any endeavor you set your mind to, even against all odds.

When I was 27 years old, many of my friends were purchasing homes. It forced me to take a hard look at my lifestyle. I wondered how it was possible they were able to do this, or more importantly, what was I not doing correctly considering I only had $26 in my savings account. It depressed me and I felt like a dismal failure.

After about a week of depression I woke one morning asking an important question of myself, "Who says I can't own a home?" It was then I realized that it was my own negative mindset that kept me from believing I could actually own a home. I made myself believe it would never happen because, as a matter of fact, I had virtually no money in the bank, and it was seemingly impossible to save the amount of money it would take to purchase a home. I was the one who had a discouraged attitude and was not allowing the positive force of faith we all have access to, to work through me.

I finally realized I had to change this faithless negative mind set to one that was more positive thinking, if I were to ever experience the joy of actually owning a home. It was a major breakthrough in my thinking. It was that final shift to positive thinking awareness that has made me realize where success comes from.

In Romans 8:5-8 Paul writes of "setting our minds" on the Spirit and not of the world.

> *For those who are according to the flesh set their minds on the things of the flesh, but those who are according to the Spirit, the things of the Spirit. For the mind set on the flesh is death, but the mind set on the Spirit is life and peace…*

I use this example to illustrate we must have a mindset on the principles of God. Having a positive mind set, is faith flowing through our hearts and permeating our mind. It is a gift from God. In Proverbs 4:23, Solomon writes, *"Watch over your heart with all diligence, for from it flow the springs of life."*

I couldn't express it any better than this. The *"springs*

of life" filled my heart and I believed in myself that I could accomplish what was once thought to be impossible.

The next day I started looking for a piece of property, found one under-valued and purchased it, fortunately without having to put any money down. Then I had it appraised. It had equity so I designed the home I wanted to build, drew up a set of plans and completed a budget of the costs to build it. This represented countless phone calls and hours of talking with people, asking "how to" questions. Then taking all this acquired knowledge, and everything else, into the bank vice president along with my new positive attitude to convince them to give me a loan. My success was in the form of a $50,000 construction loan approved by the bank and later another $25,000 for the completion of the home of my dreams and built by the sweat of my brow.

God gives us the faith to believe in ourselves, but we have to put that faith to work by doing, picking up our feet and walking, so to speak. You know, we have to get busy and do what it takes to accomplish our dreams. It won't happen sitting on the coach and waiting for something to happen; we have to get busy.

During wars throughout the history of the world, men went to battle. Those that found themselves in the midst of a battle didn't live long by thinking negatively or by being gripped by fear. They had to keep the negative thinking at bay if they were to survive to see another day. Those that didn't, found themselves cowering in a foxhole of fear and susceptible to a perceived stronger enemy and possible death.

We will be faced throughout our lives with challenges. We will have to make life changing decisions. We will all have difficulties. But through it all, we must set our hearts and minds on the Spirit, and not the world, and maintain a positive attitude if we are to experience success in all things.

The Faith of Abram (Abraham)

The story of Abram (Abraham) is one of the best faith stories of the Bible. God told him that he would have a son. He never lost faith despite the fact that through the years his wife Sarah was baron and had since passed the age of bearing children. God's promise to Abraham is found in Genesis chapter 15:4-6, some twenty years before the promise was actually realized.

> *Then behold, the word of the Lord came to him, saying, "This man will not be your heir; but one who will come forth from your own body, he shall be your heir." And He took him outside and said, "Now look toward the heavens, and count the stars, if you able to count them." And He said to him, "So shall your descendants be." Then he believed in the Lord and He (the Lord) reckoned it to him as righteousness.*

And later Abraham, at the age of 100 years, was visited by the Lord which is recorded in Genesis 18:1-14 as follows:

> *Now the Lord appeared to him by the oaks of Mamre, while he was sitting at the tent door in the heat of the*

day. When he lifted up his eyes and looked, behold, three men were standing opposite him; and when he saw them, he ran from the tent door to meet them and bowed himself to the earth, and said, "My lord, if now I have found favor in your sight, please do not pass your servant by. Please let a little water be brought and wash your feet, and rest yourselves under the tree; and I will bring a piece of bread, that you may refresh yourselves; after that you may go on, since you have visited your servant." And They said, "So do, as you have said." So Abraham hurried into the tent to Sarah, and said, "Quickly, prepare three measures of fine flour, knead it and make bread cakes." Abraham also ran to the herd, and took a tender and choice calf and gave it to the servant, and he hurried to prepare it. He took curds and milk and the calf which he had prepared, and placed it before them; and he was standing by them under the tree as they ate. Then they said to him, "Where is Sarah your wife?" And he said, "There, in the tent." He said, "I will surely return to you at this time next year; and behold, Sarah your wife will have a son." And Sarah was listening at the tent door, which was behind him. Now Abraham and Sarah were old, advanced in age; Sarah was past childbearing. Sarah laughed to herself, saying, "After I have become old, shall I have pleasure, my lord (Abraham) being old also?" And the Lord said to Abraham, "Why did Sarah laugh, saying, 'Shall I indeed bear a child, when I am so old?' Is anything too difficult for the Lord? At the appointed time I will return to you, at this time next year, and Sarah will have a son.

Sarah was about eight years younger than Abraham, at the time of the Lords' visit, which would put her at about 92 years old, well past her child-bearing years. You can see by the testimony that Sarah's faith was not that of Abraham, yet she still received the gift promised by the Lord of her first born child, a son. How amazing is that, to birth a child at the age of 92, for you see nothing is impossible with God.

What comes to mind is recorded in Mathew 19:24-26 where Jesus answered the question of His disciples. "*...then who can be saved?*":

> *And again I say to you, it is easier for a camel to go through the eye of a needle, than for a rich man to enter the kingdom of God." And when the disciples heard this, they were very astonished and said, "then who can be saved?" And looking upon them Jesus said to them, "with men this is impossible, but with God all things are possible."*

"*With men this is impossible, but with God all things are possible.*" This I find increasingly true with each passing day. Once we realize this or believe in faith then we allow our Lord to work His supernatural power on our behalf and not be restricted by our own carnal thinking. We will experience the results of His supernatural power working on our behalf, and His blessings will be on us unrestricted.

From Faith to Faith

When I was younger, I depended on my own strength to accomplish things in my life. However, as I grow older, it becomes more evident that my body is losing strength making it less able to depend on. Not only that, but as I get older, I recognize that things are out of my control, and I may feel helpless to solve a particular situation. Naturally, I cry out to God for help and I'm slowly learning to put my trust in Him for everything; it's a process. The good thing is that as I turn to Him in faith, He blesses me with increased measures of faith, just like learning to have faith in myself as a youngster. In essence this is, "from faith to faith." In Romans 1:16-17:

> *For I am not ashamed of the gospel, for it is the power of God for salvation to everyone who believes, to the Jew first and also to the Greek. For in it the righteousness of God is revealed from faith to faith; as it is written,* "BUT THE RIGHTEOUS SHALL LIVE BY FAITH."

We take this new found faith in knowing that He will work behind the scenes, even as we sleep. In Psalms 127:2, *"It is vain for you to rise up early, to retire late, to eat the bread of painful labors; for He gives to His beloved even in his sleep."*

I have come to know and accept the fact that He loves me unconditionally, even more than an earthly father could possibly love His children. Since He is the Creator of the universe, I have also come to know that with Him all things are possible. I have my human limitations and unbelief that often times keeps me from knowing His love and experiencing His blessings.

Our unbelief, just like negative thinking, will actually keep God, our heavenly Father, from working through us or for us. This is probably the biggest problem today in the Christian community. We either don't believe in God's power to be truly manifested in our lives, or not enough. We therefore depend on our own strength to deal with every aspect of our lives totally wrapped up in a worldly mindset. But instead, we should be looking to our Heavenly Father and His Son Jesus for everything, every day, all through the day, not just on the Sundays when and if we go to church.

Our Lord wants us to look to Him for everything, not just sometimes (Hebrews 12:2). If we are to experience His divine supernatural power in our lives, we must commit to Him 100 per cent. We must turn our hearts and minds toward Him to see the manifestation of His power working on our behalf every day. To Him be the Glory!

Yes, I Can Climb That Mountain

I had a vision many years ago, that was more than a just a dream. It was so real and the images were so vivid, that to this day it seems as though it just happened yesterday. Ever since that experience, I have pondered over it and tried to understand its meaning.

The vision started with me walking with an angelic figure to the base of a shear vertical cliff where there was a rope dangling down from above. He asked me, "Do you think you could climb this rope to the top?"

I looked up the approximate 100 foot cliff and with confidence responded, "Of course I can." It looked easy to me, and I didn't hesitate in my response. Within a very short while I was at the top and he was still by my side.

At the top, there was a plateau with green pastures and random trees scattered over the country side. Through the middle was a meandering stream, and there were people running, laughing and playing everywhere. However, it didn't concern me, as I instinctively and obediently followed my companion on a well worn-path that led us to the left 180 degrees and up a small outcropping of rocks. He brought me then to the base of another vertical cliff and asked, "Can you climb this cliff to the top?"

My attention was directed to another rope dangling at the base of the second cliff, and after looking up, I immediately was filled with fear and doubt as I responded to his question, "No way!" It was at least 1,000 feet straight up and looked cold and dangerous.

As it were, I then left the angelic figure, turning away from the cliff and started mingling with the people below never thinking of him again, and then I awoke. I pondered what had taken place for hours afterwards as to what it could have meant and why it happened. I was intrigued and happy for the experience, nonetheless.

After many years of wondering what the vision represented, I've come to realize that by our own strength we can accomplish much, but there are challenges that we may face that are seemingly impossible for us. You see, we know our own limitations and if we depend on our own strength, the answer is always going to be, "No way!" when faced with an overwhelming challenge. However, with God, I could have climbed that rope with ease. With God I built a home. With God all things are possible.

With God All Things Are Possible

Again, the Scripture where Jesus spoke these most powerful words to his disciples were recorded in the book of Mathew (19:26), *"With men this is impossible, but with God all things are possible."* I want you to get it! Nothing is impossible with God, so don't limit Him by thinking otherwise.

In the book of Mark, Jesus was approached by a man who had a mute son was plagued by uncontrollable convulsions, foaming at the mouth, grinding his teeth, and stiffening, all from childhood. The man cried out to Jesus and Jesus responded in Mark 9:19-27:

> *And He answered them and said, "Oh unbelieving generation, how long shall I be with you? How long shall I put up with you? Bring him to me!" And they brought the boy to Him. And when he saw Him, immediately the spirit threw him into a convulsion, and falling to the ground, he began rolling about and foaming at the mouth. And He asked his father, "How long has this been happening to him?" And he said, "From childhood. And it has often thrown him both into the fire and into the water to destroy him. But if You can do anything,*

take pity on us and help us!" And Jesus said to him, "If you can? All things are possible to him who believes."

Immediately, the boy's father cried out and began saying, "I do believe; help my unbelief." And when Jesus saw the crowd gathering, He rebuked the unclean spirit, saying to it, "You deaf and dumb spirit, I command you, come out of him and do not enter him again." And crying out and throwing him into terrible convulsions, it came out; and the boy became so much like a corpse that most of them said, "He is dead!" But Jesus took him by the hand and raised him; and he got up.

Our unbelief keeps us from realizing the full potential of our relationship with our heavenly Father. This includes not believing that people can actually be healed, but as we read, the man asked Jesus for help with his unbelief, and it was granted to him. His son was healed of the evil spirit that possessed him as a result.

Smith Wigglesworth was a great man of faith. I spoke earlier of him, but one of his healing experiences is a wonderful example of the faith and the power of God if you would only believe.

There was a man who lived in Wales, England and worked as a tin miner during the day and a preacher at night. As one might expect, he exhausted himself and contracted tuberculosis. For four years he was bed ridden and had to be fed and cleansed by others.

Two young men who were zealous for the Lord, came

from Wales to visit Smith's mission during this time. They were impressed by the good works of God at the mission and mentioned to Smith, "We would not be surprised if the Lord brings you to Wales to raise our 'Lazarus.'" They referred to the preacher as 'Lazarus,' who had been bed-ridden with tuberculosis for two years, at that time.

Smith found himself in Wales two years later and went up on a mountain top to pray with a friend who had accompanied him. While on the mountain top, the Lord spoke to him and said, "I want you to go and raise 'Lazarus.'" He told the friend what the Lord had said to him, and when they got down to the valley, He wrote a postcard to the folks who had been caring for the preacher. In the postcard he wrote, "When I was up on the mountain praying today, God told me that I was to go and raise 'Lazarus.'"

When he arrived at the place, he was greeted by a man. He looked at Smith and said, "Did you send this?"

"Yes," Smith replied.

The man replied, "Do you think we believe in this?" Here, take it," and he threw the postcard at Smith.

The man called a servant and said, "Take Smith and show him Lazarus." Then he said to Smith, "The moment you see him, you will be ready to go home. Nothing will keep you here."

Everything the man spoke to Smith was true from a human standpoint. Lazarus was nothing more than skin stretched over bones. There was no life to be seen in him. Everything about him spoke of decay.

Smith tried to get the man to believe, but he had no faith. In fact, there was no one surrounding Lazarus who believed with faith that anything could be done about his condition. However, a man and a woman asked Smith and his friend to come stay with them. Smith asked if he could count on them to help pray for Lazarus, but he told them he needed three others besides himself, his friend and them. This would make a total of seven people to pray over Lazarus.

Smith wrote about the difficulty there was in that Welsh village to get the people to believe. He was asked, "Ready to go home?"

He further wrote, "It is a blessed thing to learn that God's Word can never fail. Never listen to human plans. God can work mightily when you persist in believing Him in spite of discouragement from the human standpoint. When I got back to the man to whom I had sent the postcard, he asked, 'Are you ready to go now?'"

Smith replied, 'I am not moved by what I see. I am moved only by what I believe. I know this: no man looks at the circumstances or relies on his feelings if he believes. The man who believes God has his request.'"

In Romans 1:17, it is written, *"For in it the righteousness of God is revealed from faith to faith; as it is written, 'but the righteous man shall live by faith.'"*

Smith fasted that night. Here is the full account of his experience raising the man whom the people in that small Welsh community nick-named Lazarus:

"When I got to bed, it seemed as if the Devil tried to place on me everything that he had placed on that poor man on the sickbed. When I awoke in the middle of the night, I had a cough and all the weakness of a man with tuberculosis. I rolled out of bed onto the floor and cried out to God to deliver me from the power of the Devil. I shouted loud enough to wake everybody in the house, but nobody was disturbed. God gave the victory, and I got back into bed again as free as I had ever been in my life. At five o'clock the Lord awakened me and said, 'Don't break bread until you break it around My table.' At six o'clock He gave me these words: *And I will raise him up'* (John 6:40). I elbowed the fellow who was sleeping in the same room. He said, 'Ugh!' I elbowed him again and said, 'Do you hear? The Lord says that He will raise him up.'

At eight o'clock they said to me, 'Have a little refreshment.' But I have found prayer and fasting the greatest joy, and you will always find it so when you are led by God. When we went to the house where Lazarus lived, there were eight of us altogether. No one can prove to me that God does not always answer prayer. He always does more than that. He gives, *'... exceedingly abundantly above all that we ask or think'* (Ephesians 3:20).

I will never forget how the power of God fell on us as we went into that sick man's room. As we made a circle around the bed, I got one brother to hold the sick man's hand on one side, and I held the other, and we each held the hand of the person next to us. I said, 'We are not going to pray; we are just going to use the name of Jesus.' We all knelt down and whispered that one word, 'Jesus! Jesus! Jesus!' The power of God fell, and then it lifted. Five times the power of God fell, and then it remained. But the man in the bed was unmoved. Two years previously, someone had come along and had tried to raise him up, and the Devil had used his lack of success as a means of discouraging Lazarus. I said, 'I don't care what the Devil says. If God says He will raise you up, it must be so. Forget everything else except what God says about Jesus.'

A sixth time the power fell, and the sick man's lips began moving, and the tears began to fall. I said to him, 'The power of God is here; it is yours to accept.' He said, 'I have been bitter in my heart, and I know I have grieved the Spirit of God. Here I am, helpless. I cannot raise my hands or even lift a spoon to my mouth.' I said, 'Repent, and God will hear you.' He repented and cried out, 'O God, let this be to Your glory.' As he said these words, the power of the Lord went right through him.

I have asked the Lord to let me never tell this story except the way it happened, for I realize that God can never bless exaggerations. As we again said, 'Jesus! Jesus! Jesus!' the bed shook, and the man shook. I said to the people who were with me, 'You can all go downstairs now. This is all God. I'm not going to assist him.' I sat and watched that man get up and dress himself. We sang the doxology as he walked down the steps. I said to him, 'Now tell what has happened.'

It was soon told everywhere that Lazarus had been raised up. People came from all over to see him and to hear his testimony. God brought salvation to many. Right out in the open air, this man told what God had done, and as a result, many were convicted and converted. All this occurred through the name of Jesus, *'through faith in His name'* (Acts 3:16). Yes, the faith that comes by believing in Jesus gave this sick man perfect soundness in the presence of them all."

The important thing to note with this story is that it wasn't a man or a group of people who healed "Lazarus" in that small village; it was their faith in believing through the name of Jesus that healed him. Yet even our faith is a gift from God, as Jesus is the author and perfecter of our faith (Hebrews 12:2). To Him be the glory!

We Are No Longer Under The Law

Furthermore, it is important to understand that we are no longer under the law, as evidenced in Galatians 3:5-14:

Does He then, who provides you with the Spirit and works miracles among you, do it by the works of the Law, or by hearing with faith? Even so Abraham, "BELIEVED GOD, AND IT WAS RECKONED TO HIM AS RIGHTEOUSNESS." Therefore, be sure that it is those who are of faith who are sons of Abraham. And the Scripture, foreseeing that God would justify the Gentiles by faith, preached the gospel beforehand to Abraham, saying "ALL THE NATIONS SHALL BE BLESSED IN YOU." So then those who are of faith are blessed with Abraham, the believer. For as many as are of the works of the Law are under a curse: for it is written, "CURSED IS EVERYONE WHO DOES NOT ABIDE BY ALL THINGS WRITTEN IN THE BOOK OF THE LAW, TO PERFORM THEM." Now that no one is justified by the Law before God is evident; for, "THE RIGHTEOUS MAN SHALL LIVE BY FAITH." However, the Law is not of faith; on the contrary, "HE WHO PRACTICES THEM SHALL LIVE BY THEM." Christ redeemed us from the curse of the Law, having become a curse for us for it is written, "CURSED IS EVERYONE WHO HANGS ON A TREE." in order that in Christ Jesus the blessing of Abraham might come to the Gentiles, so that we might receive the promise of the Spirit through faith.

Bear with me on this as confusing as it might be to you, because it is deep in thought and is logically written. God used Paul to pull it all together. He explains the words and events written in the Old Testament that have now been made known to man. Paul continues in Galatians 3:15-29:

Brethren, I speak in terms of human relations: even

though it is only a man's covenant, yet when it has been ratified, no one sets it aside or adds conditions to it. Now the promises were spoken to Abraham and to his seed. He does not say, "And to seeds," as referring to many, but rather to one, "And to your seed," that is, Christ. What I am saying is this: the Law, which came four hundred and thirty years later, does not invalidate a covenant previously ratified by God, so as to nullify the promise. For if the inheritance is based on law, it is no longer based on promise; but God has granted it to Abraham by means of a promise. Why the law then? It was added because of transgressions, having been ordained through angels by the agency of a mediator, until the seed should come to whom the promise had been made. Now a mediator is not for one party only; whereas God is only one. Is the Law then contrary to the promises of God? May it never be! For if a law had been given which was able to impart life, then righteousness would indeed have been based on law. But the Scripture has shut up all men under sin, that the promise by faith in Jesus Christ might be given to those who believe. But before faith came, we were kept in custody under the law, being shut up to the faith which was later to be revealed. Therefore, the Law has become our tutor to lead us to Christ, that we may be justified by faith. But now that faith has come, we are no longer under a tutor. For you are all sons of God through faith in Christ Jesus. For all of you who were baptized into Christ have clothed

> *yourselves with Christ. There is neither Jew nor Greek, there is neither slave nor free man, there is neither male nor female; for you are all one in Christ Jesus. And if you belong to Christ, then you are Abraham's offspring, heirs according to promise.*

What this means is that the Law has become our tutor to lead us to Christ in faith. The promise by faith in Jesus Christ is given to those who believe. We are all sons of God through faith in Christ Jesus. We are all one in Christ Jesus. If we belong to Christ, then we are offspring of Abraham, heirs according to promise.

The eleventh chapter of Hebrews is known as the "faith" chapter. It is written about the faith of Abel, Enoch, Noah, Abraham, Sarah, Isaac, Jacob, Joseph, and Moses. These men and women of old had tremendous faith as we read in Hebrews 11:30-40:

> *By faith the walls of Jericho fell down, after they had been encircled for seven days. By faith Rahab the harlot did not perish along with those who were disobedient after she had welcomed the spies in peace. And what more shall I say? For time will fail me if I tell of Gideon, Barak, Samson, Jephthah, of David, and Samuel and the prophets, who by faith conquered kingdoms, performed acts of righteousness, obtained promises, shut the mouth of lions, quenched the power of fire, escaped the edge of the sword, from weakness were made strong, became mighty in war, put foreign armies to*

flight. Women received back their dead by resurrection; and others experienced mockings and scourgings, yes, also chains and imprisonment. They were stoned, they were sawn in two, they were tempted, they were put to death with the sword; they went about in sheepskins, in goatskins, being destitute, afflicted, ill-treated (men of whom the world was not worthy), wandering in deserts and mountains and caves and holes in the ground. And all these, having gained approval through their faith, did not receive what was promised, because God had provided something better for us, so that apart from us they should not be made perfect.

Jesus the Author and Perfecter of our Faith

Hard to believe, but what a gift God has given us; that through our faith in Jesus Christ and the blameless self sacrifice He made for us, we may be made perfect in the eyes of God. Paul writes in Hebrews 12:1-3:

Therefore, since we have so great a cloud of witnesses surrounding us, let us also lay aside every encumbrance, and the sin which so easily entangles us, and let us run with endurance the race that is set before us, fixing our eyes on Jesus, the author and perfecter of faith, who for the joy set before Him endured the cross, despising the shame, and has sat down at the right hand of the throne of God. For consider Him who has endured such

> *hostility by sinners against Himself, so that you may not grow weary and lose heart.*

"Jesus is the author and perfecter of faith;" this can only mean that without Jesus it is impossible for us to have faith in Him without Him. However, we play a part in all of this as well. Unless we exercise our free will and open our hearts to Him in believing in faith, He can't gift increased measures of faith back to us. To help you understand this you need to understand what Paul writes in Ephesians 1:4-6 as follows:

> *…just as He chose us in Him before the foundation of the world, that we should be blameless before Him. In love He predestined us to adoption as sons through Jesus Christ to Himself, according to the kind intention of His will…*

First, this speaks factually that we existed before our physical birth. Even if we were just a mere thought in God's mind before the earth was created, we were chosen *"in Him before the foundation of the world."*

We also read that, *"he predestined us to adoption as sons through Jesus Christ to Himself,"* and that this was, *"according to the kind intention of His will."* It is not by chance that you are reading this book. It's not by chance that you are being led to the Truth. It's not by chance that you want to know more. God knows you, He chose you, and He knows the end before it comes. He is patient for you. He loves you and He wills you for salvation to be with Him for eternity without stress, pain, anxiousness, and all the things that are not good, worldly or cause you to be separated from Him.

Can you see that? Does that make sense to you? It took me many years to come to that realization, but it is clear to me now.

Faith is rooted in Free Will

You have to remember that He gave us free will to either choose Him or reject Him. Then for us to have faith in Him, we must exercise our free will and open our hearts to the possibility of His existence that He may reveal Himself to us. This will result in His revealing Himself to us, which will give us faith to believe in Him and further trust in Him as we experience a spiritual relationship with Him for the first time.

For me it was opening the door to the possibility of Jesus' existence. I wanted to know the truth about Him; was He real or not? I asked Him to reveal Himself to me. Although it took two years, yes two years, He was faithful and revealed Himself to me to the point that now I would die for Him; yes I would gladly and willing forfeit my life to defend His name.

You may be asking yourselves why I would be willing to forfeit my life for Jesus. This can be explained by giving you an example of circumstance:

> If someone held me captive at gunpoint, and said to me "deny Jesus and live." It would be easy to deny Him and live, right? But you see, I couldn't deny Jesus even under these circumstances. His truth has

been revealed to me. How could I deny this truth and live with myself? I couldn't deny my own earthly father, for that matter, let alone denying the Creator of the universe.

Jesus gave His life for each of us. Would you give your life to save your son or daughter or loved one? I would hope the answer to that is yes. But for God, it was an easy decision to give over His son to the sons of perdition that we all may have a way out of this sin and death. Even though it was difficult for Jesus we read His account of the night he was arrested and before He was put to death. He knew what was going to happen. This is evidenced by sweating blood that night (Luke 22:44). He grieved to the point of death in His anguish. Yet He accepted the will of His father as we read of the account in Mathew 26:38-39:

> *Then He said to them, 'My soul is deeply grieved, to the point of death; remain here and keep watch with Me.' And He went a little beyond them, and fell on His face and prayed, saying, 'My Father, if it is possible, let this cup pass from Me; yet not as I will, but as You will.'*

We know that Peter believed he would not deny Him. The words of Jesus are recorded in Mathew 26:31-35:

> *Then Jesus said to them, "You will all fall away because of Me this night, for it is written, 'I WILL STRIKE DOWN THE SHEPHERD, AND THE SHEEP OF THE FLOCK WILL BE*

SCATTERED!' But after I have been raised, I will go ahead of you to Galilee." Peter said to Him, "Even if I have to die with you, I will not deny You." All the disciples said the same thing too.

The rest is history, because we know that Peter denied Him not once, but three times as Jesus had foretold. This can also be read in the other Gospels: Mark chapter 14, in Luke chapter 22, and John chapter18. Apparently, none of His disciples stood by Him or helped Him in anyway. Perhaps not as blatantly as Peter denied knowing Him, but nevertheless they abandoned Him as was prophesied in the book of Zechariah (13:7).

My heart is in the right place in believing that I would gladly give my life for Jesus. No one really knows how they will react in a similar situation as that of Peter and the other disciples. I want to believe that I would be true to my convictions, but until it becomes real, I can only hope. The fact is, all of His disciples eventually did die as martyrs because they chose not to deny His name. And let's not forget the countless millions over the course of the past 2,000 years who have suffered death to martyrdom.

For me, it is more than simply believing in Him, because I have come to have a personal relationship with Him on a daily basis. He is everything to me; I dread the thought of walking through this life without His love, strength, support, protection, help, hope, and a future eternal life with Him. Living life wrapped up in the world without Him is hopeless and will result in death…a spiritual death and one I'm not willing to forfeit so easily.

Faith Can Move Mountains

We've all heard that faith can move mountains. Here we see the words of Jesus that speaks of that kind of faith in Mathew 17:20:

> *And He said to them, 'Because of the littleness of your faith; for truly I say to you, if you have faith as a mustard seed, you shall say to this mountain, Move from here to there, and it shall move; and nothing shall be impossible to you.'*

Isn't it amazing that Jesus chose a mustard seed for the example of faith needed to move a mountain? Were you aware that the smallest seed of all seeds is a mustard seed? If we had that kind of faith, *"nothing shall be impossible to you."* Doesn't that reveal how little our faith actually is? You might be asking right now, 'How can we get that kind of faith? It seems impossible!' It is only impossible if we allow the enemy to convince us it's impossible. Did you hear that? Apparently, the vast majority of us allow the enemy to sow unbelief in our hearts.

It only requires that we believe, contrary to what words the enemy uses in our minds to discourage us and convince us that something is impossible. How is it that we can believe the lies of the enemy so easily and not the words of our Creator which are truth to the core? Believe, and you shall be set free from the bonds of the enemy. The weakness of God is stronger than the greatest strength of the enemy. You can believe in that! Jesus died to give us this power; the kind of power that totally defeated the enemy at the cross. Through the resurrected Jesus Christ, the author and perfecter of our faith we have freedom from the enemy! Hallelujah!

The enemy doesn't want us to know the truth. Keep that in mind. He wants to ride us around like a horse having a bit in our mouth to pull us this way and that way. When we realize this, we can buck him off and run free because Christ gave us this power in Him.

Fix Your Eyes on Him

In faith, let's look at the words Jesus spoke to His disciples before He ascended into heaven; words that are faith building; words that have power in them, and were recorded in John 14:13-14: *"And whatever you ask in My name, that will I do, that the Father may be glorified in the Son. If you ask Me anything in My name, I will do it."*

Ask the Father in the name of Jesus and you shall receive it! Believe it! It's as simple as that. There is power in the Word of God so read it, believe it and you shall come to realize it more with each passing day.

Faith comes from hearing and hearing by the word of Christ. Ponder that. It can be found in Romans 10:17 Paul writes, *"So faith comes from hearing, and hearing by the Word of Christ."* We know that the Scriptures are the Word of God. We also know that Jesus is the Word. If you sincerely want to know the truth and your heart is open to knowing the truth, then truth will be revealed to you and you will gain increased measures of faith in the following ways:

- By reading the Scriptures; we are expected to (1 Thessalonians 5:27; Col 4:16; Mat 12:3, 5; Mat 19:4; Mat 21:16, 42; Mat 22:31; Mat 27:37; Mar 2:25; Mar 12:10, 26; Luk 6:3; Eph 3:4;).
- By listening for the Spirit to reveal truth within the Scriptures (Luke 10:21).
- By hearing others explain the Scriptures (Luke 4:21).
- By doing not just hearing (Jam 1:25).
- By yielding your free will to knowing God's will for you (Mat 6:10).
- By fixing our eyes on Jesus, the author and perfecter of faith (Heb 12:2).

Do not waver in unbelief. That is like the surf of the sea, driven and tossed by the wind. When you ask of the Lord, believe you will receive that which you ask. Let's read the words of James who was the brother of Jesus. James, being guided by the Holy Spirit wrote in James 1:6-8:

> *But if any of you lacks wisdom, let him ask of God, who gives generously and without reproach, and it will be given to him. But he must ask in faith without any doubting, for the one who doubts is like the surf of the sea, driven and tossed by the wind. For that man ought not to expect that he will receive anything, being a double-minded man, unstable in all his ways.*

Don't be too hard on yourself if you find yourself doubting from time to time. It is not always as easy as it sounds to believe; the learning may very well be through life trials and the testing of our faith. In time, you will gain freedom from unbelief and enjoy the peace that comes from believing and trusting in our Creator, Jesus Christ, by fixing the eyes of our heart on Him.

Here is a poem of encouragement I wrote a few years ago:

GIFT OF LOVE

God divine came to the earth
He was born of virgin birth

Esteemed kings came from afar
Drawn close to Him by His star

Wisdom graced Him in His teens
Humbly, not by wealthy means

His life was tried and tested
In Him, our future vested

By evil means, He was tried
Stripped, beaten, they pierced his side

Our sins, they nailed to a tree
Painful, but it had to be

Raised now our glorious King
And with our hearts, we do sing

Faith of a Mustard Seed

Send us Your Spirit of love
To us, descend from above

In Your time, please take us home
There never to be alone _{JAG 2009}

Chapter 6

ONLY BELIEVE

The Bible teaches us that if we only believe in Jesus Christ and confess with our mouth, we will be saved. It's as easy as that. However, what constitutes belief? What does it mean to believe in Jesus Christ? One thing we do know is that to believe is done in faith. We read in Romans 10:8-10:

> "...THE WORD IS NEAR YOU," *in your mouth and in your heart—that is, the word of faith which we are preaching, that if you confess with your mouth Jesus as Lord, and believe in your heart that God raised Him from the dead, you will be saved; for with the heart a person believes, resulting in righteousness, and with the mouth he confesses, resulting in salvation.*
>
> And in verse 13, "...*for,* 'WHOEVER WILL CALL ON THE NAME OF THE LORD WILL BE SAVED.'"

The meaning of the word "believe" in the Oxford dictionary is as follows: "1. Accept as true or as conveying as truth. 2. Think; suppose. 3a. Have faith in the existence. b. Trust in as a policy."

In the Webster's dictionary we read the meaning of believe: "1. To accept as real or true. 2. To credit with veracity. 3. To expect or suppose: Think —vi 1. To have faith, esp. religious faith. 2. To have faith or confidence: Trust. 3. To have confidence in the truth, value, or existence of something."

The meaning of the word "faith" in the Oxford dictionary is: "1. Complete trust and confidence." On the other hand, Webster's dictionary meaning of faith is: "1. Confident belief in the truth, value, or trustworthiness of a person, idea, or thing."

So as you can see, the two words, believe and faith, go hand in hand in that when one believes, one must have a certain degree of faith. When speaking of faith, one must have belief.

Faith and belief are a choice made with the heart and mind. If we can get past the lies of the enemy that are whispered in our ears almost continually and make a conscious choice to turn away from the darkness into the light, truth will be revealed to us and our faith will be increased as it is written in Romans 1:17, *"For in it the righteousness of God is revealed from faith to faith; as it is written, 'BUT THE RIGHTEOUS MAN SHALL LIVE BY FAITH.'"*

In Romans 3:21-26 we see the promise of righteousness is given to those who believe in faith through Jesus, our justifier:

> *But now apart from the Law the righteousness of God has been manifested, being witnessed by the Law and the Prophets, even the righteousness of God through faith in Jesus Christ for all those who believe; for there is no distinction; for all have sinned and fall short of the glory of God, being justified as a gift by His grace through the redemption which is in Jesus Christ; whom God displayed publicly as a propitiation in His blood through faith. This was to demonstrate His righteousness, because in the forbearance of God He passed over the sins previously committed; for the demonstration, I say, of His righteousness at the present time, that He might be just and the justifier of the one who has faith in Jesus.*

The Scripture states that we are all sinners and fall short of the glory of God. The emphasis is on the word *"all." N*ot even one of us is without sin except the Lord Jesus alone.

In Acts 13:38-39 we read:

> *Therefore let it be known to you, brethren, that through Him forgiveness of sins is proclaimed to you, and through Him everyone who believes is freed from all things, from which you could not be freed through the Law of Moses.*

Paul and Silas were in prison and while there, they were praying and singing hymns praising God, while the prisoners were listening. Suddenly, there was a great earthquake and all the doors in the prison were opened; all the chains that bound them were loosed or unfastened. We read in Acts 16:27-31:

> *...when the jailer had been roused out of sleep and had seen the prison doors opened, he drew his sword and was about to kill himself, supposing that the prisoners had escaped. But Paul cried out with a loud voice, saying, "Do yourself no harm, for we are all here!"*

The Jailer was fearful, but he became so grateful that he asked Paul and Silas how he could be saved and we read the account in Acts 16:29-31:

> *And he called for the lights and rushed in and, trembling with fear, he fell down before Paul and Silas, and after he brought them out, he said, "Sirs, what must I do to be saved?" And they said, "Believe in the Lord Jesus, and you shall be saved, you and your household."*

Not only was the jailer saved, but we read that his entire household was saved for his belief. I find that so incredible, but I also find it reassuring that in my believing, I can save my entire family. Praise God!

In John 10:9-10, Jesus spoke to His disciples saying, *"I am the door; if anyone enters through Me, he shall be saved, and shall go in and out, and find pasture."*

In John 14:6-7, Jesus spoke to the Phillip saying:

> *I am the way, and the truth, and the life; no one comes to the Father, but through Me. If you had known Me, you would have known My Father also; from now on you know Him, and have seen Him.*

This also speaks to the deity of Jesus as was discussed in previous chapters, pointing to the mystery of the trinity. Phillip continued to question Jesus which was recorded in John 14:8 and asked, *"...Lord, show us the Father, and it is enough for us."* Jesus replied to him in verses 9-11:

> *Have I been so long with you, and yet you have not come to know Me, Philip? He who has seen Me has seen the Father; how do you say, "Show us the Father?" Do you not believe that I am in the Father, and the Father in Me; otherwise believe on account of the works themselves.*

To me, believing in Jesus Christ means you recognize that He is the Son of God incarnate (in the flesh), that you recognize He led a sinless life being pure and without blemish, the Sacrificial Lamb, caused to suffer and die on a cross that we might be free from all our sins and death. He rose on the third day and ascended into Heaven and is seated on the right hand of God, and through His innocent blood, we have eternal salvation. If you believe this, then you are a believer in Jesus Christ and your name is written in the book of life for all eternity.

A perfect example of this is while Jesus is hanging on the cross having a criminal on either side of Him. One of them mocks Him, and the other one recognized His innocence, His deity and speaks to Jesus to remember him when He comes into His kingdom. It can be found in the Luke 23:39-43:

And one of the criminals who were hanged there was hurling abuse at Him, saying, "Are You not the Christ? Save Yourself and us!" But the other answered, and rebuking him said, "Do you not even fear God, since you are under the same sentence of condemnation? And we indeed justly, for we are receiving what we deserve for our deeds; but this man has done nothing wrong." And he was saying, "Jesus, remember me when You come into Your kingdom!" And He said to him, "Truly I say to you, today you shall be with Me in Paradise."

This example is clear from the words spoken from Jesus Himself that if you believe, then your salvation is sure and Paradise awaits your passing from life. Jesus said, *"…today you shall be with Me in Paradise."* not tomorrow, not next week, nor at the end of the age, but today!

This reminds me of the story about Lazarus, Abraham and a rich man. The account explains the separation between those that willfully chose a worldly life ignoring God, and those that chose a Godly life living by faith. The full account can be found in the book of Luke 16:19-31. The choices we make can have everlasting consequences.

THE ETHIOPIAN EUNUCH

The disciples then left and started back to Jerusalem and were preaching the gospel to many villages along the way when an angel of the Lord spoke to Philip in Acts 8:26 saying, *"Arise and go south to the road that descends from Jerusalem to Gaza (this is a desert road)"*

Philip listened and did as the angel had said. He met an Ethiopian eunuch sitting in his chariot. For your information, a eunuch is a servant of a kingdom that was either born without testacies or was made that way purposely in order that he remain faithful in not having relations with anyone close to the royalty. This is the account of the eunuch coming to the Lord found in the book of Acts 8:27-40:

> *He arose and went; and behold, there was an Ethiopian eunuch, a court official of Candace, queen of the Ethiopians, who was in charge of all her treasures; and he had come to Jerusalem to worship. And he was returning and sitting in his chariot, and was reading the prophet Isaiah. And the Spirit said to Philip, "Go up and join this chariot." And when Philip had run up, he heard him reading Isaiah the prophet, and said, "Do you understand what you are reading?" And he said, "Well, how could I, unless someone guides me?" And he invited Philip to come up and sit with him. Now the passage of Scripture which he was reading was this:*
>
> > *"HE WAS LED AS A SHEEP TO SLAUGHTER;*
> > *AND AS A LAMB BEFORE ITS SHEARER IS SILENT,*
> > *SO HE DOES NOT OPEN HIS MOUTH.*
> > *IN HUMILIATION HIS JUDGMENT WAS TAKEN AWAY;*
> > *WHO SHALL RELATE HIS GENERATION?*
> > *FOR HIS LIFE IS REMOVED FROM THE EARTH."*
>
> *And the eunuch answered Philip and said, "Please tell*

me, of whom does the prophet say this: Of himself, or of someone else?" And Philip opened his mouth, and beginning from this Scripture he preached Jesus to him. And as they went along the road they came to some water; and the eunuch said, "Look! Water! What prevents me from being baptized?" And Philip said, "If you believe with all you heart, you may." And he answered and said, "I believe that Jesus is the Son of God." And he ordered the chariot to stop; and they both went down into the water; Philip as well as the eunuch; and he baptized him. And when they came up out of the water, the Spirit of the Lord snatched Philip away; and the eunuch saw him no more, but went on his way rejoicing. But Philip found himself at Azotus; and as he passed through he kept preaching the gospel to all the cities, until he came to Caesarea.

This account has always intrigued me. Not only were the eunuch's eyes opened to see that Jesus was the Son of God and that he was baptized in the Spirit and saved, but that Philip was snatched away to another place by the Spirit of the Lord, right before the eunuch's eyes.

All Things Are Possible to Him Who Believes

Oh, the power of the living God…we have no idea what power has been given to us through our Lord Jesus Christ if we would only believe. Through God we see in Mathew 9:23, *"all things are possible to him who believes."*

In Ephesians 1:18-19, Paul writes:

> *I pray that the eyes of your heart may be enlightened, so that you may know what is the hope of His calling, what are the riches of the glory of His inheritance in the saints, and what is the surpassing greatness of His power toward us who believe.*

Yes, that the eyes of your heart may be enlightened so that we may come to know of His power toward us who believe. We must turn our hearts toward Jesus in order to receive the increased faith and see the manifestation of His power working in our lives and receive the gift and the blessings of the Holy Spirit.

Jesus told His disciples and the other followers with them before His ascension into Heaven, *"And behold, I am sending forth the promise of My Father upon you; but you are to stay in the city until you are clothed with the power from on high."* This would be clothed with the power of the Holy Spirit, the Helper, as Jesus speaks and is recorded in John 14:12-19:

> *Truly, truly, I say to you, he who believes in Me, the works that I do shall he do also; and greater works than these shall he do; because I go to the Father. And whatever you ask in My name, that will I do, that the Father may be glorified in the Son. If you ask anything in My name, I will do it. If you love Me, you will keep My commandments. And I will ask the Father, and*

> *He will give you another Helper, that He may be with you forever; that is the Spirit of truth, whom the world cannot receive, because it does not behold Him or know Him, but you know Him because He abides with you, and will be in you. After a little while the world will behold Me no more; but you will behold Me; because I live, you shall live also.*

Most of us have no idea the power that is in the name of Jesus. For if we truly knew, the world would be changed. Not the "change" we are falsely promised by the politicians, but transforming change. Truth would prevail; people would be healed of sickness; miracles would be common place; the enemy would lose the power we give him, and hope would rule.

BY GRACE IS OUR SALVATION, THROUGH FAITH

Salvation is in the blood of Jesus. His sacrifice, His grace, is our salvation through faith. As it is written in 2 Timothy 3:15: *"…and that from childhood you have known the sacred writings which are able to give you the wisdom that leads to salvation through faith which is in Christ Jesus."*

Let's not overlook the fact that grace is freely given to us by Jesus even though we don't deserve it. It is this grace that we have salvation through faith, as written in Ephesians 2:8:

> *For by grace you have been saved through faith; and that not of yourselves, it is the gift of God; not as a result of works, that no one should boast.*

In the Nelson's, "New illustrated Bible Dictionary" the meaning of grace is defined in great detail for a better understanding:

> GRACE – favor or kindness shown without regard to the worth or merit of the one who receives it and in spite of what that person deserves. Grace is one of the key attributes of God. The Lord God is 'merciful and gracious, long suffering, and abounding in goodness and truth' (Ex. 34:6). Therefore, grace is almost always associated with mercy, love, compassion, and patience.
>
> In the Old Testament, the supreme example of grace was the redemption of the Hebrew people from Egypt and their establishment in the Promised Land. This did not happen because of any merit on Israel's part, but in spite of their unrighteousness (Deut. 7:7-8; 9:5-6). Although the grace of God is always free and undeserved, it must not be taken for granted. Grace is only enjoyed within the Covenant—and the gift is received by people through repentance and faith (Amos 5:15). Grace is to be humbly sought through the prayer of faith (Mal. 1:9).
>
> The grace of God was supremely revealed and given in the person and work of Jesus Christ. Jesus was not only the beneficiary of God's grace (Luke 2:40), but was also its very embodiment (John 1:14), bringing it to humankind for salvation (Titus 2:11). By His death and resurrection, Jesus restored the

broken fellowship between God and His people, both Jew and Gentile. The only way of salvation for any person is 'through the grace of the Lord Jesus Christ' (Acts 15:11).

The grace of God revealed in Jesus Christ is applied to human beings for their salvation by the Holy Spirit, who is called 'the Spirit of grace' (Hebrews 10:19). The Spirit is the One who binds Christ to His people so they receive forgiveness, adoption to sonship, newness of life, as well as every spiritual gift or grace (Ephesians 4:7).

The theme of grace is especially prominent in the letters of Paul. He sets grace radically over against the law and the works of the law (Romans 3:24, 28). Paul makes it abundantly clear that salvation is not something that can be earned; it can be received only as a gift of grace (Romans 4:4". Grace, however, must be accompanied by faith; a person must trust in the mercy and favor of God, even while it is undeserved (Romans 4:16; Galatians 2:16).

The law of Moses revealed the righteous will of God in the midst of pagan darkness; it was God's gracious gift to Israel (Deut. 4:8). But His will was made complete when Jesus brought the gospel of grace into the world (John 1:17).

I couldn't have explained it more thoroughly as was done here in Nelson's Dictionary. Do you realize that since the sin of Adam, the relationship with God was broken? But Jesus restored that relationship with man. We now have direct access to the Father through Jesus, just as Adam had before he sinned. When we accept His sacrifice for our sins, the Father doesn't see us as sinners any longer. He only sees His Son in us. Can you fathom that? Jesus loves us so much that He took on the suffering we deserve and paid the penalty for us in order to give you and me undeserved favor, if we only believe. Hallelujah!

BORN AGAIN OF THE SPIRIT

There is another aspect of our belief that must be addressed. You have probably heard Christians refer to "being born again." We are all born of the flesh at birth, but when you accept Christ in your heart as your savior, you are then born of the Spirit. Jesus spoke these words to Nicodemus and can be read in John 3:3-21:

> *Jesus answered and said to him, "Truly, truly, I say to you, unless one is born again, he cannot see the kingdom of God." Nicodemus said to Him, "How can a man be born when he is old? He cannot enter a second time into his mother's womb and be born, can he?" Jesus answered, "Truly, truly, I say to you, unless one is born of water and the Spirit, he cannot enter into the kingdom of God. That which is born of the flesh is flesh, and that which is born of the Spirit is spirit. Do not marvel that I said to you, 'You must be born again.' The wind blows where*

it wishes and you hear the sound of it, but do not know where it comes from and where it is going; so is everyone who is born of the Spirit." Nicodemus answered and said to Him, "How can these things be?" Jesus answered and said to him, "Are you the teacher of Israel, and do not understand these things? Truly, truly, I say to you, we speak that which we know, and bear witness of that which we have seen; and you do not receive our witness. If I told you earthly things and you do not believe, how shall you believe if I tell you heavenly things? And no one has ascended into heaven, but He who descended from heaven, even the Son of Man. And as Moses lifted up the serpent in the wilderness, even so must the Son of Man be lifted up; that whoever believes may in Him have eternal life. For God so loved the world, that He gave His only begotten Son, that whoever believes in Him should not perish, but have eternal life. For God did not send the Son into the world to judge the world, but that the world should be saved through Him. He who believes in Him is not judged; he who does not believe has been judged already, because he has not believed in the name of the only begotten Son of God. And this is the judgment, that the light is come into the world, and men loved the darkness rather than the light; for their deeds were evil. For everyone who does evil hates the light, and does not come to the light, lest his deeds should be exposed. But he who practices the truth comes to the light, that his deeds may be manifested as having been wrought in God."

Chapter 6

Once For All

He who believes in the Son of God, Jesus Christ, is not judged on the merit of their sins. Jesus paid the price for our iniquities. Our sins He sees no more. This salvation has been made retroactive, for all time, for all who believe "once for all."

We can read this in Romans 6:10, *"For the death that he died, He died to sin, **once for all**; but the life that He lives, He lives to God."*

Remember that the high priest entered the Holy of Holies just once a year for all the sins of the people. But all the priests sacrificed every day for the sins of the people as well. It was a continual ritual day in and day out, every day. We read in Hebrews 7:26-28:

> *For it was fitting that we should have such a high priest, holy, innocent, undefiled, separated from sinners and exalted above the heavens; who does need daily, like those high priests, to offer up sacrifices, first for his own sins, and then for the sins of the people, because this He did **once for all** when He offered up Himself. For the Law appoints men as high priests who are weak, but the word of oath, which came after the Law, appoints a Son, made perfect forever.*

And further in Hebrews 9:11-14:

> *But when Christ appeared as high priest of the good things to come, He entered through the greater and more*

*perfect tabernacle, not made with hands, that is to say, not of this creation; and through the blood of goats and calves, but through His own blood, He entered the holy place **once for all**, having obtained eternal redemption. For if the blood of goats and bulls and the ashes of a heifer sprinkling those who have been defiled, sanctify for the cleansing of the flesh, how much more will the blood of Christ, who through the eternal Spirit offered Himself without blemish to God, cleanse your conscience from dead works to serve the living God?*

We also read in Hebrews 10:10, *"And by that will, we have been made holy through the sacrifice of the body of Jesus Christ,* **once for all***."*

In 1 Peter 3:18 we read:

*For Christ also died for sins **once for all**, the just for the unjust, in order that He might bring us to God, having been put to death in the flesh, but made alive in the Spirit…*

CONTEND EARNESTLY FOR FAITH

In the book of Jude, we read that faith was given once for all. This is intriguing because it points to the sacrifice of Jesus as faith being bestowed through that sacrifice, but that we must, *"contend earnestly"* for that faith. Let's read the words written in the book of Jude 1:3:

Beloved, while I was making every effort to write you

> *about our common salvation, I felt the necessity to write to you appealing that you contend earnestly for the faith which was **once for all** delivered to the saints.*

In Webster's dictionary, we read that the word "contend" defined is: 1. "to struggle as in battle: FIGHT" 2. "to compete, as in a race: VIE."

Jude appeals to the body of believers to fight or strive for victory, for the faith that was delivered to the saints. This is something I don't believe I have sought after enough. Is it possible that not many of us have? Could it be that we have taken lightly the faith we have available to us? Apparently, we must "contend earnestly" for this faith, but also know it has already been given or made available to us; we need only fight for it.

In Mark 11:24 we are told that when we pray and ask for things, we should believe that we have already received them.

> *Therefore, I say to you, all things for which you pray and ask, believe that you have received them, and they will be granted you.*

What a revelation! Accept His grace and believe in faith.

Chapter 7

LOVE IS GREATER THAN ALL

Everyone has their opinion of what love is, but first let's take a look at what the definition is. The Webster's dictionary defines love as, "An intense affection for another person based on personal or familial ties." There are a myriad of other definitions, even in Webster's, but they all have to do with affection, an attraction, enthusiasm or especially sexual desire. I find it amazing that any mention of love associated with God, humankind's devotion to or adoration of God is very far down on the list.

Although we may associate certain feelings with love, in many life situations, I don't know if we will ever fully understand it. Each of us have understanding of what we think love is, but it may differ from one to another. We can at times be confused into thinking that a certain feeling, we are experiencing is love. For instance, we may feel an overwhelming sense that we find someone attractive and count that as love while others may call it infatuation. Regardless, love can be a mystery and is certainly something most people welcome when it knocks at their door.

The Scriptures tell us that the love God has for us surpasses our knowledge. In the book of Ephesians 3:19, *"...and to know the love of Christ which surpasses knowledge..."* Why is it, do you think, that we don't have the capacity to fully understand that kind of love? I think the answer to this question is, in part, because of the human limitations of our brain and the fact that we are infants compared to the knowledge of God. In reality, we may think we are more than we are. The fact remains, however, that all the knowledge man can muster is considered foolishness to God. The question remains, will we fully grasp the width, the depth and the length of love God has for us, while yet on this earth?

Let's explore further what the Scriptures have to say about love for a better understanding. They give insight into the very nature of God. The truth is, the Scriptures are the manifestation of love because it is laced all through His word.

In 1 John 4:8, we see that God is love, *"The one who does not love does not know God, for God is love."* And further in verse 16 we read:

> *And we have come to know and have believed the love which God has for us. God is love, and the one who abides in love abides in God, and God abides in him.*

We must learn to abide in His love and His love will flow

like rivers of water through our hearts and on to others. This is the hope we should be striving for that we will reflect the great love that He has for us. Paul writes in the book of 1 Corinthians 13:1-3 and makes it abundantly clear. If we do not have this love, we are but a noisy gong, even if we have all the gifts of the Spirit:

> *If I speak with the tongues of men and of angels, but do not have love, I have become a noisy gong or a clanging cymbal. And if I have the gift of prophesy, and know all mysteries and all knowledge and if I have all faith, so as to remove mountains, but do not have love, I am nothing. And if I give all my possessions to feed the poor, and if I deliver my body to be burned, but do not have love, it profits me nothing.*

Paul continues in verses 4-13, giving us a specific outline of how love is manifested in us toward others. He also reflects on the partiality of our knowledge and understanding. We may think we have love in our hearts, but how many of us actually practice love as described in these verses:

> *Love is patient, love is kind, and is not jealous; love does not brag and is not arrogant, does not act unbecomingly; it does not seek its own, is not provoked, does not take into account a wrong suffered, does not rejoice in unrighteousness, but rejoices with the truth; bears all things, believes all things, hopes all things, endures all things. Love never fails; but if there are gifts of prophesy,*

> *they will be done away; if there are tongues, they will cease; if there is knowledge, it will be done away. For we know in part, and we prophesy in part; but when the perfect comes, the partial will be done away. When I was a child, I used to speak as a child, think as a child, reason as a child; when I became a man, I did away with childish things. For now we see in a mirror dimly, but then face to face; now I know in part, but then I shall know fully just as I also have been fully known. But now abide faith, hope, love, these three; but the greatest of these is love.*

This exposes my heart as lacking in what I need most; more of God's love. When I reflect on this description of love, I miss the mark terribly. How often I'm offended by what someone says or does. It demonstrates the degree I'm still in the flesh with all its weaknesses.

Mathew recorded the words Jesus spoke to His disciples in the book of Mathew (5:43-46):

> *You have heard that it was said, "YOU SHALL LOVE YOUR NEIGHBOR," and hate your enemy.' But I say to you, love your enemies and pray for those who persecute you, so that you may be sons of your Father who is in heaven; for He causes His sun to rise on the evil and the good, and sends rain on the righteous and the unrighteous. For if you love those who love you, what reward do you have? Do not even the tax collectors do the same?"*

I don't know about you, but to love your enemy is not an easy thing. In fact, I don't think it's humanly possible. The only way we could learn to love our enemies is for God's Spirit to indwell us, giving us the ability to love others unconditionally, grace to grace.

We are commanded to love God first and foremost. Secondly, we are commanded to love our neighbor as our self. Jesus was tested by the Pharisees. A lawyer, who was also one of them, asked Jesus this question found in Mathew 22:36: "*Teacher, which is the great commandment in the Law?*"

His answer was recorded in verses 37-40:

> *And He said to him,* "YOU SHALL LOVE THE LORD YOUR GOD WITH ALL YOUR HEART, AND WITH ALL YOUR SOUL, AND WITH ALL YOUR MIND. *This is the great and foremost commandment. The second is like it,* YOU SHALL LOVE YOUR NEIGHBOR AS YOURSELF. *On these two commandments depend the whole Law...*"

Jesus quoted the Old Testament Scripture. However, when we read Deuteronomy 6:5 we see the Hebrew meaning of the words heart, soul and might:

Heart...*Lebab* = inner man, mind, will, heart
Soul...*Nephesh* = a soul, living being, life, self, person, desire, passion, appetite, emotion
Might...*Meod* = muchness, force, abundance

Here is the Old Testament Scripture in its entirety as recorded in Deuteronomy 6:5-9, we are expected to love the Lord in eventuality:

> *You shall love the Lord your God with all your heart and with all your soul and with all your might. These words, which I am commanding you today, shall be on your heart. You shall teach them diligently to your sons and shall talk of them when you sit in your house and when you walk by the way and when you lie down and when you rise up. You shall bind them as a sign on your hand and they shall be as frontals on your forehead. You shall write them on the doorposts of your house and on your gates.*

However, Jesus didn't quote the Old Testament Scripture precisely. He stated heart, soul and mind, as opposed to heart, soul and might. Jesus didn't make a mistake. Everything He did had reason. Therefore, it would be helpful to explore the Greek words to grasp the full depth of love that Jesus wants us to see:

> **Heart**...*Cardia* = denotes the centre of all physical and spiritual life; the middle or central or inmost part of anything, even though inanimate
> **Soul**...*Psyche* = the breath of life; the vital force which animates the body and shows itself in breathing; life; that in which there is life..a living being, a living soul
> **Mind**...*Dianoia* = mind as a faculty of understanding, feeling, desiring

It is obvious that Jesus wants us to love everyone, God first and foremost. It sounds easy. All we have to do is love God and then love our neighbor, right? Well what if "neighbor" means everyone, not just the person next door. Remember, He told us to love our enemy as well; even when someone is attempting to do you harm. Do you think you can do this strictly on your own without God's help? It certainly doesn't sound easy anymore.

Are We capable of Unconditional Love?

Let's read the words that Jesus spoke to His disciples about loving one another in John 13:34-35:

> *A new commandment I give to you, that you love one another, even as I have loved you, that you also love one another. By this all men will know that you are My disciples, if you have love for one another.*

The words of Jesus are quite clear. We are told, NO, commanded to love one another with unconditional love! How is that possible? This could only be possible if we have His Holy Spirit firmly rooted in our hearts. When His Holy Spirit indwells us, we are filled with His love and therefore His love passes through us to others. If you still doubt this, then read the words Jesus spoke and were recorded in the book of John (15:5):

> *I am the vine, you are the branches; he who abides in Me, and I in him, he bears much fruit; for apart from Me you can do nothing.*

Jesus tells us that even He can do nothing without the Father. So how could we possibly do anything without Him, especially if He could do nothing without the Father? Let's read the words He spoke to the Jews on the Sabbath, in John 5:17-19:

> *But He answered them, "My Father is working until now, and I Myself am working." For this cause therefore the Jews were seeking all the more to kill Him, because He not only was breaking the Sabbath, but also was calling God His own Father, making Himself equal with God. Jesus therefore answered and was saying to them, "Truly, truly, I say to you, the Son can do nothing of Himself, unless it is something He sees the Father doing; for what the Father does, these things the Son also does in like manner."*

We all have a natural capacity to love, especially, when someone does something nice for us. If you are a decent person and aspire to do what is right, you have the capacity to love built into the good that you do. Call it a reflection of good works.

We have also learned to love family members and friends in this sort of way. It is much easier when we know they are on our side and rooting for us to love them naturally. But is it truly unconditional love because this is what Jesus is asking us to do? Maybe, but most of the time it is conditional. How quickly love can turn into hate if we find out that someone has stabbed us in the back.

I hope you are getting the point I'm trying to make here. If you think about the love that you feel, how deep does it really go? Are you willing to jump into a raging river to save an individual who's been swept away with the current and facing death? I hope the answer is yes, but a great many of us would think twice before we'd risk our own life to save the life of another especially if we don't know them. I will say that in my younger days when I was in great physical shape and felt invincible, the chances of me actually jumping into rough waters were better than they are as my body ages.

This reminds me of a story of a man who was rock climbing with his son in Colorado. They were working their way up the side of a cliff. About one hundred feet or so from the bottom the son lost his balance. The father instinctively reached for him to keep him from falling, but unfortunately they both fell to their death. This was a demonstration of unconditional love beyond what many of us would have done. Personally, I want to believe in my heart that I would risk my life in a "heart beat" for not only for my own children, but for anyone. I pray that that would be the case. However, I don't think we truly know what we are capable of until the situation is presented to us in reality.

Unconditional love is maintained no matter what someone does to you personally. You are still able to love that person with that love that can only come from the God of love. If someone says something bad about you or spurned you in some way, could you love him or her as we are instructed? The answer for most of us is probably not. But that is exactly what the Lord is instructing us to do, hard as it may be. On the cross, Jesus lifted His head toward heaven and said, "Father forgive them for they know not what they do".

Another example of the love Christ wants us to have, is the account of the martyr Stephen, who was stoned to death. This can be found in the book of Acts (7:54-60). He came to know the love that God so wants all of us to have. While Stephen was being stoned, he cried out with a sincere heart in verse 60, "*Lord, do not hold this sin against them.*" Can you imagine being stoned to death and yet having love and compassion for those doing the stoning? That is where the Lord wants us to be; to love so deeply that we have no ill feelings toward our fellow man.

There is freedom and joy that comes to us when we are able to master unconditional love when the natural and worldly inclination is to hate someone who has wronged us in some way. We cannot accomplish this on our own no matter how hard we try. We don't have the power to overcome the enemy on our own without the help of God. Yes, it is the enemy that keeps us entangled in the web of hatred with anxious heart and mind. The enemy uses deception in justification and reasoning as well as our own self righteousness to keep us from extending God's love toward our enemies.

We have read that love has much to do with forgiveness. Are you a forgiving person? Is it difficult for you to be forgiving? I've learned that forgiveness may be skin deep. If we dig further, we may find that we still harbor ill feelings toward an individual. One way to know is to think of their name and discover what emotions it evokes. If we find it difficult to think of that person without reliving the pain he or she caused us, then we have not truly forgiven. This is where the power of God is needed. We need His help to overcome the strongholds the enemy has established in us.

We must turn to God and ask Him to give us the strength to forgive a person in His love. This will not be easy and will more than likely take some time and a lot of prayer. However, over time and with a sincere heart, even with little baby steps, God will grant you freedom from this bondage and replace it with the love that can only come from Him. This doesn't mean you have to go see or talk to someone who has harmed you. It only means that in your heart you will turn the hatred or dislike you have into something more pleasant; yes even to love with the love of God.

During the course of any given day, things happen to us all that cause us to send ill thoughts toward another individual. Maybe someone cuts you off on the freeway or cuts in line at a grocery store. The fact is, most of us are in our selfish mode when we are on a mission, having somewhere to go or something important to get done that day. We might have tunnel vision in order to stay focused on the task at hand. Inevitably, someone will interfere with our intended path and we may naturally tend to take it personally. This will happen more often in a busy environment where life is on a fast track.

The cold hard fact is that no matter where you live or how busy your life is, you will have negative thoughts directed toward others at sometime. It could happen while watching the news or you can become offended by something a family member says or does. I could go on and on about the possibilities that cause a discouraging or hateful thought. The fact is, it happens to us all at some time.

Some people can easily dismiss these events as trivial bumps along our path, while others take it to heart more deeply. Of course, it also depends on how offensive the event is or who is being the offensive one. We may hold some to a higher standard and thus are offended more easily. However, we have the ability to turn our thoughts toward God at those times and circumvent the painful place we tend to go when these things occur.

There are a few things that the Lord has shown me and are most helpful in coping with those times of weakness. Especially averting sinful thoughts directed toward those who directly or indirectly offend us.

First, I remind myself that God loves them the same as He loves me. When sinful thoughts come to mind, I say to myself instead, "God love them." It may not always be easy to do, but in time, it will become a habit.

The second helpful thought is a revelation that the Spirit gave to my wife. She was trying to help me cope with someone who was driving me nuts with anxiety. She explained to me I should think of them as being a horse, having a bit in their mouth, and being ridden by the enemy who is directing their path, their thoughts and their actions.

Lastly, we need to keep in mind that the person causing the offense may not be aware they are offending you. We don't know what life crisis they may be facing that day. They may have just had an argument or an illness or devastating news.

The fact is, we may never know what is affecting their adverse behavior, and we shouldn't take it personally even if it is meant to be taken personally. Be like a duck in water, and let it roll off your back.

I've got to say these analogies and thoughtful scenarios have helped me immensely in overcoming the enemy's evil thoughts that affect me at times and then get directed toward those sometimes unknowing individuals. Keeping these things in mind have made it easier for me to cope with the annoyances of life brought on by people that may not even be aware of what they are doing. The wise and healthy advice my wife reminds me often is to, "Give them grace, John. Give them grace." We are told in 1 Corinthians 16:14, *"Let all that you do be done in love."*

We are also told that if we have the love of Christ in us, it will control us. If we have the love of Christ in our hearts we no longer live for ourselves. Yes, we still have to go to work and go through the motions of life, but we are new creatures in Christ. We aspire to die to ourselves and live for Christ. Let's read the inspiring words of Paul in 2 Corinthians 5:14-21 as follows:

> *For the love of Christ controls us, having concluded this, that one died for all, therefore all died; and He died for all, that they who live should no longer live for themselves, but for Him who died and rose again on their behalf. Therefore from now on we recognize no man according to the flesh; even though we have known*

> Christ according to the flesh, yet now we know Him thus no longer. Therefore if any man is in Christ, he is a new creature; the old things passed away; behold, new things have come. Now all these things are from God, who reconciled us to Himself through Christ, and gave us the ministry of reconciliation, namely, that God was in Christ reconciling the world to Himself, not counting their trespasses against them, and He has committed to us the word of reconciliation. Therefore, we are ambassadors for Christ, as though God were entreating through us; we beg you on behalf of Christ, be reconciled to God. He made Him who knew no sin to be sin on our behalf, that we might become the righteousness of God in Him.

These are powerful words. It is clear that this is how our God wants us to live if we are to know His unconditional love. In this way, the fruit of the Spirit will be seen in us and people will be drawn to us.

We are warned against the desires of the flesh which war against the Spirit. We are told that we should live by the Spirit so that we may display the fruits of the Spirit. Let us turn to the Word of God that Paul recorded in the book of Galatians 13-26 for more insight into how we are to conduct ourselves in love:

> For you were called to freedom, brethren; only do not turn your freedom into an opportunity for the flesh, but through love serve one another. For the whole Law

> *is fulfilled in one word, in the statement, "YOU SHALL LOVE YOUR NEIGHBOR AS YOURSELF." But if you bite and devour one another, take care lest you be consumed by one another. But I say, walk by the Spirit, and you will not carry out the desire of the flesh. For the flesh sets its desire against the Spirit, and the Spirit against the flesh; for these are in opposition to one another, so that you may not do the things that you please. But if you are led by the Spirit, you are not under the Law. Now the deeds of the flesh are evident, which are: immorality, impurity, sensuality, idolatry, sorcery, enmities, strife, jealousy, outbursts of anger, disputes, dissensions, factions, envying, drunkenness, carousing, and things like these, of which I forewarn you just as I have forewarned you that those who practice such things shall not inherit the kingdom of God. But the fruit of the Spirit is love, joy, peace, patience, kindness, goodness, faithfulness, gentleness, self-control; against such things there is no law. Now those who belong to Christ Jesus have crucified the flesh with it's passions and desires. If we live by the Spirit, let us also walk by the Spirit. Let us not become boastful, challenging one another, envying one another.*

We are also told not to love the world and the things in the world. Let's read the warning of living a worldly life which was written in the book of 1 John (15-17):

> *Do not love the world, nor the things in the world. If anyone loves the world, the love of the Father is not in*

him. For all that is in the world, the lust of the flesh and the lust of the eyes and the boastful pride of life, is not from the Father, but is from the world. And the world is passing away, and also its lusts; but the one who does the will of God abides forever.

To put it simply, our choice is "Worldly versus Godly." Are we going to continue living a life being led by the world and its lusts or are we going to turn to God and live in His love and do His will? God is love; the world is anything but love.

Further in the book of 1 John (3:10-24) we get more clarification, insight and instruction. We see the representation of love in Jesus who laid His life down for us, the unworthy. We are told that we should do the same for our brothers. It's straight forward and does not parse words as we read:

By this the children of God and the children of the devil are obvious: anyone who does not practice righteousness is not of God, nor the one who does not love his brother. For this is the message which you have heard from the beginning, that we should love one another; not as Cain, who was of the evil one, and slew his brother. And for what reason did he slay him? Because his deeds were evil, and his brother's were righteous. Do not marvel, brethren, if the world hates you. We know that we have passed out of death into life, because we love the brethren. He who does not love abides in death. Everyone who hates his brother is a murderer; and you know that no murderer has eternal life abiding in him. We know love

> *by this, that He laid down His life for us; and we ought to lay down our lives for the brethren. But whoever has the world's goods, and beholds his brother in need and closes his heart against him, how does the love of God abide in him? Little children, let us not love with word or with tongue, but in deed and truth. We shall know by this that we are of the truth, and shall assure our heart before Him in whatever our heart condemns us; for God is greater than our heart, and knows all things. Beloved, if our heart does not condemn us, we have confidence before God; and whatever we ask we receive from Him, because we keep His commandments and do the things that are pleasing in His sight. And this is His commandment, that we believe in the name of His Son Jesus Christ, and love one another, just as He commanded us. And the one who keeps His commandments abides in Him, and He in him. And we know by this that He abides in us, by the Spirit whom He has given us.*

We are told in 1 John 4:1-3 that we are to test the spirits to know whether they are from God because there are many false prophets who have gone out into the world. The Lord tells us that every spirit who confesses that Jesus Christ has come in the flesh is from God. And every spirit that does not confess Jesus is not from God.

The Lord assures us that if we have God in our hearts that, *"…greater is He who is in you than he that is in the world."* He gives us further assurance that we may be able to judge the spirits of the world as follows in 1 John 4:5-6:

> *They are from the world; therefore they speak as from the world, and the world listens to them. We are from God; he who knows God listens to us; he who is not from God does not listen to us. By this we know the spirit of truth and the spirit of error.*

We must have God's love in our hearts to understand that God is love and that love is from God. Everyone who loves is born of God and knows Him. God's love was manifested in us by His Son coming into the world so that we might live through Him. Whoever confesses that Jesus is the Son of God, has God abiding in him, and he in God.

There is no fear in love. Perfect love casts out fear (1 John 4:18). We love, because He first loved us (1 John 4:19). The one who believes in the Son of God has the witness in himself, and the witness is this: God has given us eternal life, and this life is in His Son. He who has the Son has the life. This is the confidence which we have before Him. If we ask anything according to His will, He hears us.

The following is a poem I wrote in 1998 to help myself remember that God loves us unconditionally. How easy it is for us to fall victim to the wiles of the enemy that keep us hating our brothers and sisters. I recalled actual situations that for many of us are common to everyday living. It's not always easy to love them after being attacked in some way, but that's what our Lord wants from us.

GOD LOVES EM

She was rude and spoke sarcastically.
Her fury aimed directly at me.
Retaliation was on my mind,
but something much greater made me see.

At work there was a conspiracy.
I the victim, unable to be,
Revenge justified for me to find,
but something much greater made me see.

He was cool, arrogant and haughty,
his nose was in the air facing me.
Disliking was embraced toward his kind,
but something much greater made me see.

Prideful were his ways used commonly,
among the masses and sometimes me.
Their eyes were not used, forever blind,
but something much greater made me see.

That God is loving, relentlessly.
All of His children like you and me.
Remember His love for all mankind,
And in His time, He will help you see. JAG 16 Aug 98

Chapter 8

FREE WILL: A GIFT OF LOVE

There is no love like the love of the Father toward us. He made each one of us in His likeness, yet individually we are different like night and day. Not one of us are quite like another; we are unique to ourselves alone.

That is the beauty of creation. Not one animal is exactly like another. Not one flower, nor one rock or one bug either. Not one fish is exactly like another, a bird, a cloud, not even one snow flake is exactly like any other. The differences may be difficult at times to see, but they are there. Everything in this world has uniqueness, and for that matter, you can extend that to the entire universe and even to the angels.

To demonstrate His love for us, He gave us free will to either choose Him or reject Him. It reminds me of the fictional story about a toy maker who loved the puppet he created so much that when, by an act of God, it came to life, he allowed it to have free will. That toy as I'm sure you've guessed was Pinocchio. Our heavenly Father feels the same way about us as that little toy maker did about his Pinocchio.

Our free will allows us to live without any thought for the God that created us. However, if you're anything like me, when we get ourselves in over our heads we cry out, "Abba Father!" It's human nature. But as soon as we get our feet back on the ground, off we go head-long into a worldly life style without the thought of God in our lives again. For many, we may think of Him on Sunday, especially if we go to church. But for the most part, He is not an active part of our lives. Then we wonder why we have emptiness in our heart, or we are unsatisfied with our lives for one reason or another, we just are not happy about the way our lives are going. Oh, we may have wonderful days or have a great and exciting experience that puts a smile on our face, but deep down, we seem to be missing something and can't quite put a finger on what that something is.

Remember, it's the good things that happen in our lives and the good people we meet along the way that keep us going. If it was not for those good times, those good people, or the good things in our lives, life would not be pleasant. You can't deny that if you remove ALL the "good" from this life, it would surely be hell. You see, we have an obvious representation of what it would be like if there was an absence of good right here in our own life experience. Now, think of eternity and living in the absence of good—that would be hell in the truest sense of the word because there would be no light, only darkness.

We are fortunate to have free will to lead the kind of life we want to. We are also blessed to live in the United States which gives us the freedom to do as we please without government intervention. We can live wherever we want, work for whomever we choose, and go anywhere we would like without the government stopping us and limiting our freedom of movement.

The freedoms we enjoy in this country are unlike any other free nation in the world. Where citizens gain their freedoms from men, but can be revoked at any time for any reason. Our founding fathers, on the other hand, made sure the freedoms we enjoy were God given and not man given. Our political leaders would have us believe otherwise that the freedoms we enjoy are "man given" and they have the right to make laws that diminish those freedoms. That is not the way our founding fathers intended it to be.

We have also become complacent about our freedoms and have taken them for granted; we really have no idea how good we have it. We have become like spoiled children. Couple our God given freedoms with our God given free will, and we are truly free to go and do as we please here in the United States—within the guidelines of our civilized laws, of course. However, many people don't have the freedoms we take for granted here. They live under the leadership of cruel dictators, or communist rule where the state owns everything and controls everyone. And let's not forget about the forms of government that are strictly ruled by religious leaders, like in the middle Eastern countries. Most Americans selfishly turn a blind eye to see the hardships that most people on earth are living under.

When I was a child running through the woods of upstate New York, I was free. I could go and do whatever I wanted within the guidelines set by my parents. But to me, I was free. I remember climbing to the top of the tallest trees in the forest perched at the top of a hill and looking out over the expanse of the countryside. Rolling hills of deciduous forest and fertile valleys with some cleared for dairy farms or apple orchards. Although I was isolated, living in the country many miles from the nearest town, I was also blessed to have the freedom to grow up amongst nature, come to know it, learn respect for it and not fear it.

It's the kind of balance we should have in our adult lives. The experience I had as a child has helped form me to be the person I've become as an adult. Sure, there are things I look back on with regret, but for the most part when I reflect back, I have come away with much more than I may have lost by not living in the city. A respect for life and nature, a learned confidence in myself and in my abilities, a respect for others, and a humble respect for the awesome power of God, invisible as He is, yet being visible in His creation, I not only enjoyed my freedoms and free will, but came to respect them in thankfulness toward God for them.

The Scriptures are quite clear about what God wants us to do with our free will. He wants us to willingly surrender to Him, to trust in Him completely, and to die to ourselves living completely for Him. He wants communion with us every day, throughout the day reflecting on Him. Jesus set the example for us while he was here on earth and did nothing that was not His Father's will.

Jesus knew what His purpose was in life. He experienced death in order to live, not for Himself, but it was the master plan to foil the plans of the enemy and give us eternal life. Jesus knew what His death would be like, how horrific it would be, becoming sin, for the entirety of creation. From the very first sin, Adam's sin, to the last sin before the day of Jesus' return, He died for all our sins, "Once for all." Can you imagine how terrible it must have been for Him to be taking on all the sin of the world, for which He was innocent? Think about all the horrible things people have done to each other and to themselves. Take the sin in your life, for example, and how it makes you feel. Now think about everyone's sin throughout the history of mankind. Simply put, it would be the worst kind of torture one could ever imagine even if it were possible to.

The anguish Jesus faced at the garden of Gethsemane was incredibly difficult. We read in Mathew 26 that He was deeply grieved and distressed to the point of death. In Luke, it is recorded that His sweat was like drops of blood, giving us further insight into His suffering and how difficult it was for Him. His own words were recorded in each of the gospels of Mathew, Mark, Luke, and John. Jesus, knowing what He was facing, willingly gave up His free will to do the will of the Father. We read His Prayers from Mathew 26:36-46:

> *Then Jesus came with them to a place called Gethsemane, and said to His disciples, "Sit here while I go over there to pray." And He took with Him Peter and the two sons of Zebedee, and began to be grieved and distressed. Then He said to them, "My soul is deeply grieved, to the point of death; remain here and keep watch with Me." And He went a little beyond them, and fell on His face and prayed, saying, "My Father, if it is possible, let this cup pass from Me; yet not as I will, but as you will." And He came to the disciples and found them sleeping, and said to Peter, "So, you men could not keep watch with Me for one hour. Keep watching and praying that you may not enter into temptation; the spirit is willing, but the flesh is weak." He went away again a second time and prayed, saying, "My Father, if this cannot pass away unless I drink it, Your will be done." Again He came and found them sleeping, for their eyes were heavy. And He left them again, and went away and prayed a third time, saying the same thing once more. Then He came to the disciples and said to them, "Are you still sleeping and resting? Behold, the hour is at hand and the Son of Man is being betrayed into the hands of sinners. Get up, let us be going; behold, the one who betrays Me is at hand."*

Jesus freely surrendered His will to the Father knowing what He would have to go through on our behalf. He did this without the support of His disciples, for they all fell asleep. Even when He was arrested, they were not to be found. In fact, Peter denied knowing Him three times as was foretold by Jesus. While yet hanging on the cross, Jesus cried out, *"My God, My God, why have You forsaken Me?"* We see here that God the Father turned His back on His Son because Jesus represented the sin of the world. He took all of the sin of the world on His shoulders, not just part of it, but all! His suffering and life sacrifice were freely given to us in order to free us from the bondage of sin. Praise God! He now lives and is seated at the right side of the Father giving us free access to the Father, free access into the Holy of Holies that was once only permitted by the high priest once a year.

Giving up our free will, sounds like a tall order. It may seem like He is asking too much of us. I mean, we have the little things we like to do, and if we turn it all over to God we might think our lives will be dull and boring being severely restricted lacking in many things. That is normal thinking for those of us who are selfishly living in sin and enjoy that type of life style. We don't readily give it up so easily. However, on the surface it may sound like we're giving up a lot, but in actuality we gain much more than we lose.

God wants to bless us. He loves us with more love than is comprehensible by our feeble minds. Those of us who are parents and take our parenting seriously have a glimpse of what that love is like. We truly don't have a clue to the depth and width and breadth of His love until we experience the infilling of His Spirit into our hearts. Then and only then can we understand His love and come to know that God is love.

Knowing God's love is when something goes wrong on

your car, for instance, and you're stranded on a jeep trail in the middle of the Wyoming wilderness, but it doesn't bother you because you know He is with you. It's the kind of love that when you look at a dirty and sickly homeless person, you feel compassion and want to help instead of judging about the filth and disease you see before you. It's the kind of love that when you look at anyone who walks by you, no matter how they are dressed or what life style they portray, you have warmth in your heart for them, just as the Father loves us in the same way. Can we love on our own like that without the help of the Holy Spirit? No, it's not possible! The only way it is possible is by the Holy Spirit infilling our hearts and being manifested in our lives.

How is it possible for the Holy Spirit to come into our hearts and reside there? We have to ask Him to come into our hearts totally, willingly and submissive, with no fear, no hesitation and with no indecisiveness. That may be the difficult part about it, but it is where we must be in order for the healing of our heart to take place and for us to be born again into the Spirit. We must be able to accept the sacrifice that Jesus made for us. Allow His grace (undeserved favor) to wash away our sin being made clean by His blood. His Spirit will come into our hearts with a love that will fill so completely that you will gush tears of repentance, and then tears of acceptance. Those tears will turn into tears of thankfulness beyond expression and finally into tears of joy.

The power of the Spirit living within you amounts to joy like you've never known. Who wouldn't gladly give up a worldly natural life if they only knew how good it could be to be filled with His Spirit? You will have a new direction; you will have new purpose. You will have a new perspective, and you will have a newness that will be visible to all. Without speaking a word, they will know there is something that is new and different, and they will be drawn to you and will want it for themselves.

God Wants Us to Live for Him

Let's turn to the Scriptures that speak about the temporal versus the eternal things. In 2 Corinthians 5:1-7, and verses 14-15 and 17-21, we read about our bodies being earthly tents longing for our heavenly bodies. However, we have been given the Holy Spirit as a pledge of what is to come when we die to ourselves and live for Him becoming new creatures in Christ having accepted His sacrifice:

> *vv 1-7; For we know that if the earthly tent which is our house is torn down, we have a building from God, a house not made with hands, eternal in the heavens. For indeed in this house we groan, longing to be clothed with our dwelling from heaven, inasmuch as we, having put it on, will not be found naked. For indeed while we are in this tent, we groan, being burdened, because we do not want to be unclothed but to be clothed, so that what is mortal will be swallowed up by life. Now He who prepared us for this very purpose is God, who gave to us the Spirit as a pledge. Therefore, being always of good courage, and knowing that while we are at home*

> *in the body we are absent from the Lord—for we walk by faith, not by sight…*
>
> *vv 14-15; For the love of Christ controls us, having concluded this, that one died for all, therefore all died; and He died for all, so that they who live might no longer live for themselves, but for Him who died and rose again on their behalf.*
>
> *vv 17-21; Therefore if anyone is in Christ, he is a new creature; the old things passed away; behold, new things have come. Now all these things are from God, who reconciled us to Himself through Christ and gave us the ministry of reconciliation, namely, that God was in Christ reconciling the world to Himself, not counting their trespasses against them, and He has committed to us the word of reconciliation. Therefore, we are ambassadors for Christ, as though God were making an appeal through us; we beg you on behalf of Christ, be reconciled to God. He made Him who knew no sin to be sin on our behalf, so that we might become the righteousness of God in Him.*

In 2 Corinthians 4:16-18 we read further that what is seen is temporal, but what is not seen is eternal:

> *Therefore we do not lose heart, but though our outer man is decaying, yet our inner man is being renewed day by day. For momentary, light affliction is producing for us an eternal weight of glory far beyond all comparison,*

while we look not at the things which are seen, but at the things which are not seen; for the things which are seen are temporal, but the things which are not seen are eternal.

What is the "inner man" spoken about here in the Scriptures? In order to understand this, we have to look back into the Old Testament. The Hebrew word is "Leb" or "Lebab" referring to the heart. These similar Hebrew words are identical in meaning and give insight into the meaning of what the heart is: inner man, mind, will, heart. That was a revelation to me in understanding the Scriptures. Our inner man is comprised of mind, will and heart.

Paul also speaks of it being renewed day by day. That can only happen if we are in union with Him daily, reading His word and reflecting on all things in a daily relationship with Him. That may be praying to Him, thanking Him, or listening to music that is based in His knowledge all through the day. We may be working or busy doing whatever, but our inner man is singing praise to Him. I find myself singing praise and worship songs when I wake in the middle of the night, in the morning or throughout the day.

YET MAKE YOUR REQUESTS KNOWN

The Holy Spirit has given us the knowledge in the Scriptures to come to the Father in prayer, just as Jesus did while He walked the earth. The Father wants us to come to him for all our needs. He will listen to our requests and grant them in accordance with our faith. However, in Mathew 18:19 Jesus tells us:

> *Again I say to you, that if two of you agree on earth about anything that they may ask, it shall be done for them by my Father who is in heaven.*

This has been a faith builder for me because the Scripture states, *"...that if two people agree...it shall be done for them..."* It doesn't state, "if two people have faith, it shall be done for them." So when my wife and I pray together and are in agreement, whatever we pray for will be done for us by our heavenly Father. The Father has never failed to honor our prayers, and this has been a testimony to our children. To Him be the glory!

Jesus also taught us another way we should pray. In Mathew 6:5-13 we read the recorded words that Jesus spoke to His disciples with instructions of how we should pray:

> *When you pray, you are not to be like the hypocrites; for they love to stand and pray in the synagogues and on the street corners so that they may be seen by men. Truly I say to you, they have their reward in full. But you, when you pray, go into your inner room, close your door and pray to your Father who is in secret, and your Father who sees what is done in secret will reward you.*
>
> *And when you are praying, do not use meaningless repetition as the Gentiles do, for they suppose that they will be heard for their many words. So do not be like*

them; for your Father knows what you need before you ask Him. Pray then in this way;

*Our Father who art in heaven,
Hallowed be Your name.
Thy kingdom come.
Thy will be done,
On earth as it is in heaven.
Give us this day our daily bread.
And forgive us our debts, as we also have forgiven our debtors.
And do not lead us into temptation, but deliver us from evil.
For Thine is the kingdom and the power and the glory forever.
Amen.*

We have free will, but our God wants us to trust in Him and follow the path of His will. He knows exactly what is best for us and what experiences we need to learn. The sooner we recognize this, the sooner we will be in His will leading the life He has planned for us.

He is a patient God. He knows your heart and is patiently waiting to fill it with His love. Just know that He is with you as you walk, and He will be with you every step of the way even when you fall. Don't expect perfection. We all are imperfect and fall short, but know He is right there by your side to lift you up, dust you off, and guide you through it all.

www.ingramcontent.com/pod-product-compliance
Lightning Source LLC
LaVergne TN
LVHW051118080426
835510LV00018B/2109